THE ROOTS OF EXPERIENCE

Robert C. Walton

THE ROOTS
OF EXPERIENCE

and its interpretation by
science, history and
religion

SCM PRESS LTD
BLOOMSBURY STREET LONDON

FIRST PUBLISHED 1965
© SCM PRESS LTD 1965
PRINTED IN GREAT BRITAIN BY
BILLING AND SONS LTD
GUILDFORD AND LONDON

CONTENTS

PREFACE

An author rarely knows in full the genealogy of his work. When, as in this book, the theme is our common everyday experience, it is wellnigh impossible to trace out all the branches of the tree. How many of my thoughts, I wonder, have their origin in events, situations, encounters, conversations which have long since been forgotten?

I can, however, pin-point the central stem of the family tree. For the past twenty years I have been concerned with religious education, first with the Student Christian Movement in Schools, and then with the School Broadcasting Department of the BBC. The lively challenge of young people in different kinds of schools has made me aware of two things: first, that there is an urgent need to relate the Christian religion to their general studies, particularly science and history; and secondly, that the starting point of any serious discussion with our generation cannot be an appeal to any kind of religious authority, whether camouflaged or overt. The only common ground is our universal human experience. The book, however, is not expressly written for young people or for their teachers, though some of them may find it helpful. The rejection of religious authority on the one hand; a growing dissatisfaction with knowledge chopped up into little pieces on the other; these are two of the characteristics of our contemporary intellectual life. The book, therefore, is addressed to anyone who thinks that it is important to look for a meeting place between scientists, historians and men of religion.

I can trace out also some of the branches of the tree. There are books which have directed my thinking and friends with whom I have talked and argued. Three friends, in particular, have put me deeply in their debt by reading the book in draft form, though they are not necessarily committed to its argument and certainly not responsible for its errors. They are M. A. C. Warren, Canon of Westminster, Nat. Taylor, a scientific colleague, and David Hughes, a friend of long standing. My greatest debt, however, has been to my wife, who has shared her experience with me, who has so often listened patiently whilst I thought aloud, and then, with perfect timing, has interjected 'Yes, but . . .' None the less, though I can recognize the central stem and some of the branches, the genealogical tree still remains obscure because as Tennyson wrote in *Ulysses*, 'I am a part of all that I have met'.

R.C.W.

INTRODUCTION

'WE don't believe in God, we live by reason.' This parting shot was fired by an irate suburban householder at the retreating back of a too persistent evangelist who had invaded his garden on a Sunday morning. The sentence, however, does not mean quite what it says. We do not use the formal tools of reason, which are logic and mathematics, when handling our problems, making our decisions and organizing our lives. 'Reason', for us, is the product of experience. It is, of course, experience accumulated over many years, and, in part, transmitted experience, gained from other men. It is also *interpreted* experience, which has been made to yield its meaning and has been organized into some kind of pattern.

To live by reason means also to reject authority, especially authoritarian religion which appeals, whether in a crude or in a sophisticated manner, to doctrines and standards of behaviour which are held to be binding upon us. To appeal to the 'Word of God', or to the words of scripture, or to the traditions of the Church, or to the demand which faith makes upon us is, in effect, to break off communication with twentieth century people, whose slogan might well be the caption inscribed on one of Goya's etchings: 'when reason dozes, monsters come to life.'

It is the last of these authorities which is the most formidable road-block. 'The arch sin of faith', said C. J. Jung, 'is that it forestalls experience.' Even in those types of theology in which experience is made the point of departure, faith is usually a hidden kind of authority. Professor John Baillie in his Gifford Lectures for 1961-2, published post-humously, argued that 'the proper name of religious experi-ence is faith . . . religious experience, if it is authentic, already contains faith'. He added that 'we cannot make ourselves believe and we should not try . . . faith is the gift of God'.[1] In this argument faith has the status of an authority, but for modern man faith, like doubt, is the fruit of experience.

Professor Baillie regarded the religious encounter as a special kind of experience, given to a special sort of human consciousness with which only the privileged are endowed. 'We cannot make ourselves believe . . . faith is the gift of God.' Thus at the outset religion is isolated from the other activities of life. The door is shut with a bang because so many in our world, who have been given experience, have not been given faith.

The argument of this book is that in religion, as in every other human activity, we live by interpreting the experi-ences which, in principle, can be shared by all men. Religion is the fruit of 'reason' in the suburban householder's use of the word. This does not imply the complete rejection of authority and of the faith which trusts in authority, either in religion or elsewhere. A child lives and gradually comes to know by experience. It also lives and learns by authority. This adult authority is, however, of two kinds. There is the authority which arbitrarily imposes habits of thought and behaviour. There is also the authority which explains to the child his own encounters with the world by sharing experi-ence with him. The intelligent answer to the child's reiter-ated question, 'Why?' is nearly always a passing on in a suitable form of adult experience. When in adolescence and manhood we doubt and rebel we do not, as a rule, reject our

[1] J. Baillie, *The Sense of the Presence of God* (1962), pp. 64-5.

experiences nor the authority which explains by sharing experiences, but only that other authority which arbitrarily imposes standards and beliefs upon us. The demands of faith, the Bible, the creeds, the traditions of the Church will never again be accepted as authorities with binding force upon men. They may have greater power as records of shared experience.

> I call you servants no longer; a servant does not know what his master is about. I have called you friends because I have disclosed to you everything that I heard from my Father (*John* 15.15).

Modern man, now come of age, need not quarrel with that.

The argument of this book, however, explores deeper issues than the suburban householder is likely to have contemplated. It is, in the main, a study of the way in which scientists, historians, and men of religion (especially of the Christian religion) encounter experience and interpret it. The limitation of the subject to these three disciplines is, no doubt, due in part to the limitations of my own knowledge, but none the less the choice is deliberate. Science and history are not in conflict. Indeed, in some respects they are related subjects. There is, for example, a direct link between evolutionary studies, the work of the pre-historians, and the field of the historians. Yet the experiences which come to scientists are, in important ways, different from those given to historians, and these differing experiences inculcate distinctive attitudes which can make understanding difficult. Science and Christianity, on the other hand, have often quarrelled in the past, and I believe it to be quite false to pretend that there remains no area of conflict. Again, it is by no means easy to reconcile the biblical interpretation of events with the kind of interpretations which we find in other history books. Christians ought to be deeply concerned both with nature and with history, but the wide gulf of incomprehension separating them from their contemporaries is spanned by no bridge. Many Christians today, like the Cabots of Boston, talk only to God'.

We are beginning to see how much has been lost in the fragmentation of our knowledge, and how illuminating a dialogue between us could be. A fruitful discussion, however, depends upon the participants being able to stand alongside one another, not only with sympathy, but also with understanding. That is why a large part of this book is a layman's attempt to understand how the minds of scientists and historians work, what problems they have to solve and what methods they employ. The meeting point, if there is one, is in the fact that scientists, historians and men of religion live *by interpreted experience*. For this reason I am concerned with the way in which scientists encounter phenomena as they pursue their researches, rather than with science as technology; with the experience of historians rather than with the events of the past, and with the meaning of our human situation rather than with theology.

There is a second reason for concentrating upon these three aspects of the subject. I write as a Christian, and both science and history are of especial importance for modern Christianity. Science now dominates our advanced civilizations, and in reaching that position of pre-eminent power it has thrown down challenge after challenge to traditional theology and has won every round of the contest. Yet scientific *experience* and religious *experience*, seen in depth, are not as far apart as we suppose. I shall argue in this book that there are significant connecting rods between them.

Historical experience also has firm links with religious experience, or at least with Christian experience, for 'Christianity is a religion of historians'.[1] Its scriptures are, in the main, historical documents. Its centre is not in some philo-

[1] Marc Bloch, *The Historian's Craft* (1959), p. 4.

sophical theory or theological doctrine, but in a sequence of events which happened in a country which can be visited today, at a time which, within a few years, can be accurately dated. All Christians need to share in some degree the historian's experience if they are to understand and make their own what the source books of their religion are saying to them.

Science, history and religion are not concerned with separate fragments of human experience. It is the aim of scientific philosophy 'to organize the whole of experience into a rationally connected system'.[1] There can be a history of anything from plumbing to the Papacy and between, say, a history of administration and a history of costume there may well be significant connections. Equally with science and with history, religion claims for itself the full range of human experience. There is, in principle, no encounter with the world which may not hold within itself an encounter with God. We all share an intellectual need to create conceptual schemes that may bring order into our experiences. Within our separate studies we search for patterns and relationships in order that our many and varied encounters in the world may be coherently interpreted.

[1] H. Dingle, *The Scientific Adventure* (1952), p. 203.

I

VARIETIES OF EXPERIENCE

SOMETHING happened to me. That is the simplest definition of an experience.

'I saw a light.' 'I heard a sound.' 'I tasted this substance.' 'I detected a pungent odour.' 'I felt the surface of this material.' These are the sort of experiences on which the scientist builds his interpretation of nature.

'I picked up this broken piece of pottery in the ruins of ancient Jericho.' 'I walked over the fields at Market Bosworth.' 'I visited a village church and saw the wall paintings.' 'I handled a document in the Public Record Office.' By means of such experiences the historian discovers the past.

'I went to church for a service of Holy Communion. Kneeling at the altar rail I looked at the crucifix, heard the priest's words and tasted the bread and the wine.' In such an experience the Christian draws near to the centre of his religion.

Each of these encounters with the world is a sense experience. Something happened to me through one or more of my five senses. It is the most universal and the most fundamental type of experience. It is given to the infant at his mother's breast, to the child exploring cot and play-pen, nursery and garden. It is given to all men as they move about the world and engage in everyday affairs. It is given also to the research scientist as he pursues an elaborate investigation, and to the historian as he searches for evidence of the past.

Sight, hearing, smell, taste and touch are our five windows on the world.

Experience through the senses is not, however, the only way in which we encounter the universe. There are many experiences, some of which yield factual knowledge, in which sense impressions are minimal and not the heart of the encounter.

One test case is the mathematician who claims to deal with factual propositions as well as with systems of ideas. Working out a problem in his head he does not need confirmation of his answer from any of his five senses. There are relationships within nature which can be grasped by the mind and expressed by equations, and to experience them in no way depends upon sense observation. For example, a mathematician may construct mentally a system of relationships based on measurements of electrical forces. It may be possible and desirable to verify this mental construction by sense observation and experiment, but the mathematical concept has its origin in the mind itself and is not derived from sense experience. Mathematicians indeed insist upon this even though it leads to a disagreement with philosophically minded physicists. Einstein said on one occasion:

> I do not consider it right to conceal the logical independence of the fundamental concept from the sense experiment. The connection is not comparable to that of soup to beef, but more to that of the cloakroom ticket to the overcoat.[1]

The historian is a scholar whose business is with factual knowledge. On the basis of his evidence he says that this battle was fought, this king crowned, this rebellion crushed, this policy pursued. He does not witness the battle or the coronation, does not hear the swords of the rebels, or listen to the arguments about policy. Of course someone heard the policy discussion. Possibly he told another who told a third,

[1] A. Vallentin, *Einstein* (1954), p. 55.

who instructed his clerk to write it down, and the clerk's paper has been preserved for the historian to read. Yet the transmission line from the man who heard the discussion to the historian who reads the clerk's note is too long for the original experience of hearing voices to have much significance. When the historian picks up his document it is a minor element in his experience.

There are also many encounters in which sense impressions are a pathway to the experience but do not constitute the experience itself. 'I heard a symphony.' The audible sounds made by the bows being drawn across the violins and cellos, and by the flutes and trumpets being played are not the heart of the experience. They are a pathway along which we travel to share in the end the composer's vision. This vision is not, of course, a factual proposition, but neither is it merely a high sounding noise. It is an experience of the world and by listening to the symphony we participate in it. The composer shares with us what was given to him.

When we are in love the physical presence of the other is central to the experience : separation is a deprivation, even an agony. There are moments in such a relationship when the senses entirely dominate the experience, overwhelming everything else. Yet, if the bond between the lovers is close and permanent, there are other moments equally real, equally precious, when the senses are no more than a pathway to an identity of purpose, a sharing of hopes and fears, a participation in each other's inner life, which is the heart of the experience. There are other personal relationships too in which the senses play a quite subordinate role. What we know of a person does not necessarily originate in sense impressions, though transmitted by them. We work and play and argue with colleagues and friends and it would be a thin experience indeed if we never saw them face to face, but we do not, as a matter of fact, talk about 'their well-loved features'. Here personalities are engaged together, minds are interlocked in co-operation or in conflict. And if a man loves God he loves that which eye has not seen nor ear heard.

The simple definition of an experience—'something happened to me'—must now be extended. The original meaning of the word suggests the act of going or passing through something, for instance, opening a door and entering a room. A continuous stream of experience is presented to us but we also actively seek encounters with the world. We take the initiative: 'Let's go and see what happens to us.' We deliberately expose ourselves to experience whenever we travel, read books, or visit a cinema, theatre or museum. This is what the religious man does when he devotes time and energy to prayer and worship. The same purpose prompts the historian to visit the site of a battlefield, as G. M. Trevelyan tramped over the fields of Sicily before writing *Garibaldi and the Thousand*. When a scientist sets up apparatus in his laboratory and carries through an experiment, he deliberately causes something to happen to him at a time, and in a way, of his own choosing. The French phrase for performing an experiment, *faire une expérience*, neatly makes the point.

INTERPRETING EXPERIENCE

We live by experience and sometimes we can rest content in the bare sensation. We can enjoy the relaxation of a hot bath, or take pleasure in the colours of a sunset, without feeling any compulsive need to reflect upon what is happening to us. For the most part, however, our experiences have to be interpreted. The bare experience is dumb; it must be made to speak. 'I saw a light: it came from a star.' 'The piece of pottery I found in Jericho was made in northern Mesopotamia round about 1800 BC, and suggests that in the time of Abraham there was commercial traffic between Palestine and the land of the two rivers.' 'When I went to church, knelt at the altar and tasted the bread and the wine, I was in the presence of God.' These interpretations may be true or false. We may be wrong about the star, or the date of the pot, or the presence of God, but the scientist's theory, the historian's reconstruction, the religious man's affirmation are all attempts to find meaning in their different encounters.

When we are interpreting our experiences we may consult an authority, seeking guidance by sharing in another man's encounter. If we see a light which we think comes from a star, we may try to identify the star by turning to a book on astronomy. We may compare the piece of pottery with the illustrations in Kathleen Kenyon's *Digging up Jericho*. We may examine our interpretation of our experience in church in the light of Isaiah's vision in the temple at Jerusalem (6.1-8). No scientist hesitates to accept guidance from the work of Galileo, Newton, Darwin or Einstein. A chemist studying the behaviour of gases does not, as a rule, think it necessary to repeat the standard experiments made by Joseph Priestley in the eighteenth century. He is content to rely upon Priestley as an expert witness: an authority.

This, indeed, is one of the uses of history. G. J. Renier has argued that individuals live by remembering their past experiences, and societies must do the same. Yet

> societies have not the same facilities as individuals for the auto-matic recall of past experiences. They have no organic memory that can store experiences and produce them when required. That is why, from time immemorial, men have had to tell each other and their descendants the narrative which keeps their experiences available for comparison as a preliminary to unusual action. The narrative of past experiences, active and passive, is for societies what memory is for their individual members.[1]

[1] *History: its Purpose and Method* (1950), p. 19.

This quotation brings out the point that for the historian the record of the past is not a binding authority which may not be questioned, but a sharing of experience. It is 'the narrative which keeps their experiences available for comparison'. For the same reason the scientist values the authority of the past, but if a chemist entertains any serious doubt concerning the accuracy of Joseph Priestley's conclusions he will repeat the experiments in his twentieth-century laboratory. Most Christians, ignoring dogma and theology, use their bibles as historians and scientists use the past, as a record of experience. For instance, they read and sometimes memorize verses from the psalms because they have encountered experiences similar to those of the Hebrew poets, and find meaningful the psalmists' interpretation of the experiences. In what sense the Bible can be regarded as 'revelation' is discussed later in this book. What is important, at this stage of the argument, is that the authority of scripture, like the authority of science and of history, is the authority of shared experience.

When we today interpret a light as coming from a star, or identify a piece of pottery as being of Mesopotamian origin, we are treading well-worn paths. There are moments, however, when the interpretation of experience involves a break with the past and becomes a new creation. Consider the work of a great artist. He usually begins with sense experience. He observes, maybe, a sea shell, or the flight of a bird, a scene on Blackpool beach, or the face of a woman. Then this observation rubs up against other experiences stored in the artist's memory and is transmuted by that strange alchemy which we call reflection. It begins to take a new shape as imagination works upon it. Finally the experience, long reflected upon, is recreated in sound or words, in paint or stone. A work of art is never merely a representation of what the artist once saw with his eyes. It is 'a fragment of nature which, not without loss or gain, has been filtered through the nature of one man'.[1]

The great creative scientists and historians, the great prophets of religion, are always men who recognize and exploit a whole new range of possibilities. They reshape our ideas about an aspect of the world, giving a new interpretation to old and familiar experiences; an interpretation which has been filtered through their own nature. They often do this by making odd associations between familiar experiences, combining commonplace events into a new pattern. Isaac Newton may or may not have been sitting in the garden of his mother's farm in Lincolnshire thinking about the moon when an apple fell to the ground, but he saw the significant connection between the two events. Many people before Newton had wondered what keeps the moon in its orbit. Many more had seen apples fall. The theory of gravitation was born when Newton brought together in an odd association the two quite different experiences of seeing the moon riding in the sky and the apple falling to the ground.

This chapter began with elementary examples of sense experience. It then examined other encounters in which the senses are no more than a pathway to experience, or play such a minor role that they can be ignored. Does experience become less authentic as it moves away from sense experience? The answer is 'no'. If something indeed happened to me, if I sought and found, then the experience cannot be challenged. The mathematician solving a complex problem without sense observation or verification by experiment; the moment of vision given to a composer, and our sharing in that vision as we listen to his music; the quiet world in which two people participate in each other's inner life, are all experiences as authentic as that of seeing a light. We only encounter a fragment of the totality of experience which

[1] Max Friedlander, *On Art and Connoisseurship* (n.d.), p. 26.

might be ours : we limit deliberately our encounters when we specialize, but, in principle, everything that happens to us is significant and every experience is indubitable.

Is the interpretation we give to our experience less solidly grounded than the experience itself? Plainly the answer to this question must be 'yes'. So long as we rest in the experience we are in an impregnable fortress. When we seek its meaning we are in an open battlefield where we may be challenged and forced to defend ourselves, and may possibly suffer defeat. The tension may be within ourselves. We struggle with the imprecision of words, envying meanwhile those scientists whose experiences can be precisely formulated in mathematical equations. To explain an experience, even to oneself, is often to drain away its rich and satisfying flavour : the best travel diary is a shadowy record of the journey. It is an even harder task to share the experience and its meaning with others. The interpretation we give may seem to other men inadequate, wrong or wilfully perverse. There is unity and concord so long as we rest in our own experience; division and argument when we attempt to interpret what happened to us.

The fact that the interpretation is less solidly grounded than the experience is not due solely to the difficulties of making ourselves understood, and to the alternative explanations which others may give. To interpret experiences, whether it be in science, history, religion or any other activity, we must first make a pre-supposition, a pre-rational judgment. There is no logical link leading inexorably from experience to meaning. 'I saw a light : it came from a star.' How in our thought do we move from the light to the star? The experience of seeing light is indubitable : the star, which we say is the origin of the light, can be doubted. How do we know that there are stars? 'I was at a service of Holy Communion. I tasted the bread and the wine, and I was in the presence of God.' How do we move from the sense experience to the affirmation of the divine presence? These are fundamental questions. To give even a partial answer we must examine in some detail the experience of scientists, historians and men of religion.

2

THE SCIENTIST'S EXPERIENCE

SCIENCE as an intellectual activity is a philosophy interpreting experience. 'A scientific statement must, directly or indirectly, express experience and be subject to the test of experience.'[1] This means, primarily, those encounters which are presented to us through the five senses. Observation is the major technique of the scientist. 'Go and look, and measure what you see' is his cardinal injunction.

Only that which is practically observable, that is only that which would be observable if we were able to use known means of observation to the known limits of their possibilities, is significant. Our description of the universe must describe nothing else, must imply nothing else, must imply the possible existence of nothing else.[2]

Professor Dingle in this quotation, as elsewhere in his writings, pushed the doctrine to its extreme limit. He was sharply challenged by the mathematicians because, as we have seen, observation through the senses plays so minor a role that it can usually be ignored. In Dingle's view they are reduced to the status of lab-boys. None the less, sense observation is the rock foundation upon which scientific achievement has been built. Samuel Taylor Coleridge once declared that it is essential for the achievement of abstract thought 'to emancipate the mind from the despotism of the eye'.[3] Science is built upon the opposite conviction. All

[1] H. Dingle, *The Scientific Adventure* (1952), p. 10. [2] *Ibid.*, p. 228.
[3] Quoted from A. Arber, *The Mind and the Eye* (1954), p. 119.

theories must in the end be brought to the test of sense experience.

The primacy of evidence obtained through observation over authority however venerable, was the real point at issue in the seventeenth-century quarrels between scientists and those philosophical churchmen who were committed to the teachings of Aristotle. For example, Galileo's *Dialogue Concerning the Two Chief World Systems* is a spirited attack upon knowledge derived merely from philosophical dogma, and a passionate defence of experience and reflection as pathways to truth. We may illustrate his basic argument (as well as his polemical method) by quoting an anecdote from the *Dialogue* about a famous surgeon in Venice, who demonstrated by an anatomical dissection the source and origin of the nerves in the brain. A Peripatetic philosopher (who stands for Galileo's Dominican and Jesuit opponents) witnessed the demonstration. When challenged, he replied, 'You have made me see this matter so plainly and palpably that if Aristotle's text were not contrary to it, stating clearly that the nerves originate in the heart, I should be forced to admit it to be true.'[1]

Philosophical churchmen no longer pronounce on questions of anatomy, nor do they appeal to the Bible to settle scientific questions, but the cardinal issue is not yet settled. So long as religious faith forestalls experience, so long as there is in the religious argument a point of departure and a final court of appeal which is a dogmatic authority, so long will the scientist find the argument suspect from the start by reason of his training and the long history of his craft.

Scientists would not have created a wholly new picture of the universe, nor provided the means for building a totally different kind of civilization merely by looking at the natural world with the naked eye, listening with the un-

[1] Galileo Galilei, *Dialogue* (tr. Stillman Drake, 1953), p. 108.

aided ear, and dipping the tip of a finger into a chemical substance and pronouncing it bitter. They have passed through a host of unsuspected doorways by inventing instruments which enable them to extend the range of their experience. The microscope, the telescope and the camera are familiar examples of instruments which extend the powers of seeing. The microphone and the amplifier increase the range of our hearing. The atomic physicists have gone very far indeed in their endeavour to extend their experience. One of their characteristic techniques is to disturb matter in its natural state by using some degree of violence. In a typical experiment of this kind alpha particles are used as a kind of offensive weapon to bombard a target, which is some form of matter. A third element in such an experiment is a detector which identifies and describes the objects which emerge from the bombardment. There are times when the kingdom of nature suffers violence and the violent take it by force.

A second characteristic of the scientific method is that of giving precision to experiences by means of measurement. 'I saw a light' is, to a scientist, merely a slipshod remark. A scientific statement of this experience would be in the following form: 'I observed a light of "i" intensity; its position was "p", the velocity "v". The time was "t" precisely.' Such a series of observations can be formed into an equation which summarizes a sense experience with precision.

Scientific experience based upon observation, experiment and measurement is universal: that is, it is available, in principle, to everyone. That is why an essential part of a scientist's task is the publication of his results. He must share experience with others. This does not mean, of course, that anyone can use alpha particles to bombard matter. Only a trained observer—or rather a team of observers—with access to the necessary equipment can do that. But scientific experience is public and repeatable. A trained research worker in Tokyo can repeat an experiment first performed in Amsterdam and published in a scientific journal, and obtain precisely the same results. If he does not something is wrong either with his own experiment or with the original one in Amsterdam, and he will not rest until he has tracked down the discrepancy. It is the precision of measurement, allied with the public and repeatable nature of scientific experience, which seems to give to it such certainty and authority compared with those personal and private experiences on which religious people so often rely in argument; experiences which come and go, which are outside our control; experiences which are given to some people but not to others.

INTERPRETING SCIENTIFIC EXPERIENCE

Experience only becomes meaningful when it is interpreted. This, as Francis Bacon saw, is as true of scientific experience as of any other.

> Those who have handled sciences have been either men of experiment or men of dogmas. The men of experiment are like the ant; they only collect and use: the reasoners resemble spiders, who make cobwebs out of their own substance. But the bee takes a middle course; it gathers its material from the flowers of the garden and of the field, but transforms and digests it by a power of its own. Not unlike this is the true business of philosophy; for it neither relies solely or chiefly on the powers of the mind, nor does it take the matter which it gathers from natural history and mechanical experiments, and lay it up in the memory whole, as it finds it; but lays it up in the understanding altered and digested.[1]

The purpose of observation, experimentation and measurement is to gather together and to express with precision all

[1] *Novum Organum* (1620), book 1, aphorism 95. By 'philosophy' Bacon meant what we call natural science.

the available facts about a given situation. This collection of data is, of itself, without meaning. It must be transformed and digested by the understanding. The initial step in this transformation is the adoption of an hypothesis which is a provisional interpretation, a tentative statement about the significance of the phenomena : an attempt to say what the facts mean.

Observations and experiments are not usually made at random, just to see what will happen. There are fashions in scientific ideas, and the scientist often begins with his hypothesis—with a creative idea, a 'hunch', a flight of the imagination—and he usually has a pretty shrewd idea of the kind of data which will follow from his research. But he needs confirmation or refutation of his notion and above all he needs precise measurements and statistical evidence. When the data has been assembled it must be correlated with other known and demonstrated facts which appear to be relevant. The results of many observations and experiments are thus linked in a general scheme. Then the reasoning moves from this general assembly of related facts to a wider conclusion which passes beyond the original experience to its interpretation. This is the hypothesis.

As an example we may consider an astronomer who when observing a particular star may see, as its light passes through the spectroscope, a black line across the yellow band. This may suggest to him the presence of sodium in the constitution of that star since in other observations sodium gives that characteristic black line at that point on the spectroscope. The observation will be checked time and time again. The precise position of the green band will be determined with the greatest possible accuracy. Similar observations about the chemical constitution of the stars, and dissimilar observations, if they exist, must be taken into account. Only after this intense effort is it possible to take the first step in the making of an hypothesis and state that one chemical element in the constitution of a certain star is sodium. This statement can then be related in a series of ever widening hypotheses. It may lead finally to the significant conclusion that the chemical constitutions of the stars and of the earth are comparable and have the same structure of matter. The hypothesis may then be extended still further as evidence accumulates and suggest that the universe is an organic unity. If the hypothesis justifies its place within this larger field of scientific knowledge, and stands up to the testing of many observations and experiments by scientists working independently, it may be given improved status as a scientific theory.

There is one further step. The theory may in time become a scientific law. Laws in science are not definitions of the way in which nature must behave. They are not 'laws which never can be broken' which 'for their guidance He has made'. They are statements about experience which are so well grounded, so rigorously tested, so reliable in making predictions, that only a major breakthrough would challenge them, as Einstein's theory of relativity has challenged at certain points Newton's law of gravitation.

The patient observation of facts; the carefully controlled experiments frequently demanding the construction of ingenious instruments of research; the precise measurements, the mathematical equations which so neatly summarize our knowledge; the hypotheses, theories and laws—these are not the whole of scientific experience. More important than all these is the scientist's vision; his discernment of the overall structure of nature, his intuitions that *this* is the way in which the universe is constructed. Those who have discerned relationships between the falling apple and the moon in the heavens, or between the ammonite fossilized in the Cambrian rocks and the living creatures that inhabit the earth today, and those who move with such confidence and firm step in a four dimensional universe, are men and women of creative imagination, holding in their minds a conception of a vast interlocking pattern of nature.

SCIENCE AND PHILOSOPHY

The greater number of scientific discoveries do not lead to problems of philosophy. Another antibiotic drug, an advance in the manufacture of plastics, a new theory concerning genes and chromosomes raise no awkward questions about the theory of knowledge or the structure of reality. There are some branches of science, botany for example, where concept-making is negligible: there are others, atomic physics, astronomy and evolutionary theory, which are highly conceptualized. It is modern physics, and in particular the study of the fundamental particles, which has challenged old interpretations of scientific experience, and destroyed the mechanistic model of the universe. Whilst technology advances by leaps and bounds, the philosophers of science grapple in a new form with problems which are as intractable as they are ancient.

It is now nearly forty years since Sir Arthur Eddington startled his audience assembled for the Gifford Lectures by commencing with a contrast between two tables: the familiar table of the kitchen or the living-room, 'solid and substantial', as we say, and the scientific table which is 'mostly emptiness. Sparsely scattered in that emptiness are numerous electrical charges rushing about with great speed; but their combined bulk amounts to less than a billionth of the bulk of the table itself.'[1]

Here is a glimpse of the experience of nature which is given to the atomic physicist. Matter, the very stuff of the universe, which seems so solid and reassuringly tangible,

[1] *The Nature of the Physical World* (Everyman ed., 1947), p. 6.

turns out on analysis to have nothing substantial about it. It is mostly empty space pervaded by electrical fields of force. The physicist's world is a world of fundamental particles, of which some hundred different kinds have been identified, some negative, some positive, some unstable and liable to transformation. These particles are not microscopically small, hard, round pellets. It is totally misleading to speak of them, as popular writers on science sometimes do, as 'the basic building blocks from which the entire universe is made'. What is their nature? From one point of view they are simply concepts which are to the physicist what the letters of the alphabet are to the grammarian, or numbers to the mathematician. This is a shadow world in which Eddington's shadow elbow rests upon a shadow table and his shadow pen writes the Gifford Lectures on shadow paper. Here in this strange world of atomic physics, particles which no man has ever seen, appear to be moving at a high velocity and meeting in violent collisions, and these collisions are the major clue to what is happening. The physicist, therefore, has conceived brilliantly imaginative experiments and has designed complicated apparatus to compel the fundamental particles to reveal themselves. There is, for example, the scintillation screen on which an alpha particle creates a flash of light visible through a microscope of high power at the point where it hits the screen. There is the bubble chamber filled with a liquid (often liquid hydrogen) that is above boiling point but is prevented from boiling by imposed pressure. (The technique is similar to that used in a domestic pressure cooker.) A fast particle running through the chamber causes boiling along its path, and the boiling bubbles can be observed and photographed. A third method is to use a photographic emulsion (similar to a fine grained photographic plate). This is placed in the path of fast moving particles, left for a time, and then processed in the usual way. The tracks of the particles can be seen and measured under a microscope. In all these experiments it is not the particles themselves but their tracks which can be observed, as if one were frequently coming across footprints but never saw a foot. Only up to a point, by bubbles, tracks and traces, do the fundamental particles reveal themselves and make their presence known, and for science the point is a crucial one. Beyond it the particles conceal themselves as mysteriously as any *deus absconditus*, and hide their reality from us.

All this sounds so mysterious and remote from everyday experience that we may feel that it might well be left as the private playground of atomic physicists. But it is of interest and concern to all men. For one thing it has produced in our time atomic energy and the atomic bomb. Moreover, if we are concerned, as Christians certainly ought to be, with getting to the roots of things, then it is highly important to understand that all natural phenomena run back in the end to this strange world of particles. This leads, incidentally, to some queer situations for other kinds of scientist and indeed for us all. Consider what a natural historian, say a lepidopterist, is doing. He is catching butterflies, and identifying and classifying them. His world is one in which he has direct experiences through the senses. There is the first swift identification as he perceives the colour and markings of the insect; and later the more precise classification according to form and structure. This does not appear as an insubstantial world; butterflies are not symbols and shadows, even though they sometimes seem as frail as gossamer. The lepidopterist and his net, the Scarlet Admiral and the leaf on which it rests have substance. Both hunter and hunted live, reproduce their kind and die. They are, we say, real things in a real world. Yet as we push the analysis further the reality and the substance dissolve into the shadows and symbols. The naturalist and his net, the butterfly and the leaf are all composed of atoms, and atoms can be analysed into their constituent fundamental particles. Once again we are back in that world which is mostly emptiness, thinly inhabited by particles. For the physicist, though not for the naturalist, the butterflies have gone. The mathematical equations have supplanted them.

Here is a world which it is possible for men to use for their own purposes, one that has put enormous power into their hands, but it is a shadow world which it is impossible to think and speak about if we continue to use the old concepts. To describe it as some sort of vastly complicated machine will not do. It is not a 'material' world in any sense in which the word 'materialistic' is used in science, for the classical scientific tests for the existence of a material body break down when applied to the fundamental particles.

These classical tests were described by Galileo more than three hundred years ago.

> No sooner do I form a conception of a material or corporeal substance, than I feel the need of conceiving that it has boundaries and shape; that relative to others it is great or small, that it is in this or that place, and in this or that time; that it is moving or still; that it touches or does not touch another body; that it is one, few or many; nor can I, by any effort of imagination, dissociate it from these qualities.[1]

Until the development of particle physics, a scientist confronted by the statement 'x exists' followed Galileo and asked three questions. Has 'x' mass? Has it velocity? Has it extension in space, that is, does it occupy a definite position which can be located and fixed by measuring instruments? These were the scientific tests of the reality of a material object, and if these conditions could not be fulfilled the scientist would say that he had no means of verifying the statement 'x exists'. Yet in modern atomic physics these are

[1] Quoted from A. C. Crombie, *Augustine to Galileo* (1952), p. 393.

precisely the conditions which cannot be fulfilled; at least simultaneously. A particle may have a measurement of position or it may have a measurement of velocity, but it cannot, in an exact sense, have both. This is the principle of indeterminacy. The phrase 'in an exact sense' is important. Approximate measurements are possible, but this is not good enough for science.[1] The reason for the indeterminacy is that the particles cannot be observed. They are known only through the light they emit, or the bubbles they form, as they move at high speed. So, to quote Bertrand Russell's summary of the situation:

> If you know where you are, you cannot tell how fast you are moving; and if you know how fast you are moving, you cannot tell where you are. This cuts at the root of traditional physics in which position and velocity are fundamental. You can only see an electron when it emits light, and it only emits light when it jumps, so that to see where it was you have to make it go elsewhere.[2]

The fundamental particles are at the roots of things but we have no reason whatever for describing them as material objects. Though a great deal is known about their properties and behaviour they are best described at present as events presented to our experience.

The study of the fundamental particles also raises in an acute form that ancient philosophical problem which makes the interpretation of experience so much less solidly grounded than experience itself. No man has seen a particle at any time; only the flash of light on the scintillation screen, or the tracks and traces in a bubble or cloud chamber, can be observed and measured. What justification is there, then, on strictly scientific grounds, for moving from the flash of light to postulate the existence of a particle?

[1] See A. Eddington, *The Nature of the Physical World*, pp. 216f., for an elaboration of this point.
[2] *The Scientific Outlook* (1949), p. 96.

B

This, however, is not the heart of the problem. The question may be asked of the whole of scientific experience, indeed of all sense experience. How can we be certain that there is a connection between the sense experience and the material object? The experience of observing tracks and traces in a bubble chamber is indubitable: so is the experience of a sensation of light as we look at a scintillation screen. But to say that these sense experiences have their *origin* in invisible particles is to interpret the evidence in a way that is not undeniable. It is an axiom of science that only that which is observable is significant. Thus if a scientist refuses to accept the existence of phenomena which he cannot observe then, since the fundamental particles are unobservable and cannot be shown simultaneously to possess both velocity and position in space, he must deny all knowledge of an objective physical world. If, on the other hand, he admits into his scheme of things a phenomenon which is unobservable in principle, has he any defence against a drunken man who asserts that a pink rat is sitting on his table? Science has an inescapable obligation not to go beyond the evidence, and therefore scientific idealists, like Professor Herbert Dingle, have asserted that questions about 'things in themselves' and 'actual occurrences' are meaningless because it is impossible to answer them. We must reject naïve realism and stop picturing an objective universe which exists independently of our thought of it. 'The universe is a mental construct formed to give rational coherence to our observations.' 'There is no independent universe to know.'[1]

It is a conclusion which sounds absurd. Are we really expending a vast amount of time, energy and money on research into the nature and properties of a physical universe which does not exist? There is, of course, an easy way out which all of us take, whether or not we are scientists. There

[1] *The Scientific Adventure*, pp. 233-4.

may be a philosophical doubt as to whether the fundamental particles exist, but the techniques of electronics flourish. The cathode ray tube in the television set works admirably. There may, or may not, be an objective world to know, but the farmer who can develop a new strain of wheat giving a high yield per acre will make handsome profits. Yet the experience of that shadow world of the fundamental particles, high-lighting an old problem of philosophy, has revolutionized the scientific interpretation of the universe, destroyed old concepts and suggested new ones. It is the reason why the philosophical problem attracted the attention of a man like Einstein who, when asked whether there is reality outside us, replied : 'Yes, I believe there is.' Anyone who gives a different answer and lives by it must dwell in an ivory tower. Einstein made a pre-rational judgment. He committed himself to an intellectual act of faith, arising out of tested experience, but one which, on strictly scientific grounds, can be challenged.

It is the scientific experience of the shadow world of particles which, more than anything else, has passed the death sentence upon materialism—that dreary view of the universe which saw all phenomena, even the human consciousness, as if they were nothing but elaborate, self-motivating machines. For now the whole notion of 'matter' is vague, if not meaningless. In accurate writing the very word must be written in inverted commas.

> 'Material' particles are only *states* of disturbance—but a disturbance in an unidentifiable medium, without substance. There is no substance left in physics, only form. We have the grin, but not the cat.[1]

We shall, of course, go on using 'materials' like stone, wood and metals to build our cities and construct our

[1] Heinz Posts, 'Individuality and Physics', in *The Listener*, Oct. 10, 1963.

machines, but when we reach down to the roots of things what we find can only be cautiously described as a complex pattern of events presented to our experience. Some philosophical scientists have ventured further, though they have been compelled to use analogies to express their thoughts :

> To my mind, the laws which nature obeys are less suggestive of those which a machine obeys in its motion than of those which a musician obeys in writing a fugue, or a poet in composing a sonnet. The motions of electrons and atoms do not resemble those of the parts of the locomotive so much as those of the dancers in a cotillion.[1]

This is a strange new world, but its climate is one in which a religious man can breathe.

[1] J. H. Jeans, *The Mysterious Universe* (1930 ed.), p. 136.

3

THE HISTORIAN'S EXPERIENCE

CYRIAC of Ancona, employed by Cosimo de' Medici to travel in the East in search of ancient manuscripts, left Florence on one occasion with the words, 'I go to awake the dead'. The task of the historian is indeed 'the resurrection of that which happened once'.[1] By their knowledge, imagination and mastery of the evidence they say to past events, 'Lazarus, come forth!' They speak of the fascination of this task, of 'the subtle enchantment of the unfamiliar'. 'It was so sweet', wrote the German historian Ranke, 'to revel in the wealth of all the centuries, to meet the heroes face to face, to live through everything again.'[2]

It is clear that in many respects the experience of historians differs from that of the natural scientists. Historians are concerned with 'that which happened once', but natural scientists, unless they are geologists or archeologists, are concerned with recurrent events. Cardinal Wolsey died in Leicester Abbey on November 24, 1530. The event is recorded in most history books on the Tudor period, but it is of no interest to scientists simply because it only happened once. If, however, every prominent ecclesiastic who passed through Leicester were to die there, the event would cease to have historical importance and become instead a first-class scientific prob-

[1] G. J. Renier, *History : its Purpose and Method*, p. 224.
[2] Quoted from G. P. Gooch, *History and Historians of the Nineteenth Century*, p. 73.

lem, for science is concerned with phenomena which are continually repeated.

It is one of the techniques of the scientist to conduct experiments in which events in the past are made to occur again in the present. No historian can do this: he cannot repeat the experiment. The Pilgrimage of Grace took place in the last few months of the year 1536, but no modern historian was present to see with his own eyes the standard bearer carrying Robert Aske's banner with the five wounds of Christ, or to hear with his own ears the proceedings of Aske's trial at York. There can be no direct and immediate observation of the revolt or of the trial. The Pilgrimage of Grace cannot be reproduced as a modern chemist can reproduce in his twentieth-century laboratory one of Priestley's classic experiments on the behaviour of gases. History deals with unrepeatable events: it is the resurrection of that which happened once. That is why the historian, in Marc Bloch's words, 'is as if at the rear of a column, in which the news travels from the head back through the ranks'.[1]

HISTORICAL EVIDENCE

The historian, like the scientist, often begins with an hypothesis; a creative idea, an inspired guess. Then, like Francis Bacon's bee, he must 'gather material from the flowers of the garden and the field'. He must establish the facts with precision and in detail, and as he searches for the facts the interpretation of them begins to grow. The interpretation directs the quest for the evidence, and the evidence shapes the interpretation. So the historian must ask repeatedly, What actually happened? Who said what, and when and where? Who did this deed, gave this order, planned this course of action, and who else was present and what part did they play in the sequence of events? And as

[1] *The Historian's Craft*, p. 51.

the interpretation begins to take shape the question 'Why?' becomes ever more insistent.

The historian's experience as he seeks to answer these questions may be, in some small part, sense experience, given to him chiefly through sight and touch, for an event in the past may leave 'tracks' or 'traces', as an invisible particle leaves bubbles. These 'tracks' or 'traces' (the terms seem to be borrowed from the language of the nuclear physicists) are of many different kinds. Aerial photography has revealed lost villages and pre-historic earthworks. There are historical buildings from Stonehenge to the Regency terraces of Bath. Egyptian pottery of the eighteenth century BC found in Palestine is a 'track' of the frequent coming and going of men of the land of the Pharaohs to the land of the Canaanites. A Roman copper coin of the Emperor Domitian set in the mast step of a first-century Roman ship, discovered in 1963 in the mud of the Thames near Blackfriars Bridge, is a trace of Roman contacts with Britain. An official's seal or a nobleman's coat of arms; a Saxon cross, a rusty suit of armour, or a fourteenth-century brass in a village church of a knight fully accoutred—all these are 'material' traces of the past. They can be seen and handled like geological specimens or chemical substances. A 'track' or 'trace' may, however, be non-material. The beliefs of Christians concerning the resurrection of Christ, an institution like the English Parliament or the Royal Society, a custom like the explosion of fireworks on November 5, a traditional ceremony such as the Trooping of the Colour, are all gateways back into the past.

This kind of evidence is invaluable for periods far distant from our own. For the Roman occupation of Britain, for example, the exploration of an archeological site is likely to prove more rewarding than diligent reading of Roman literature. The nearer we come to our own time the less historians are dependent upon such 'tracks' and 'traces' of a bygone civilization. In Britain official archives have been kept from the outset of the thirteenth century. An historian whose field of study is later than the twelfth century therefore works mainly with documents. In one sense these are material 'traces', but their importance lies in the testimony they offer. These documents may be State Papers recording the policies and the administration of rulers. They may be Chronicles narrating the events of the time seen through the eyes of a contemporary and intended for publication. They may be family correspondence like the medieval *Paston Letters*, or diaries like the one which Parson Woodforde kept so assiduously in the eighteenth century.

Whether the evidence comes from 'tracks' and 'traces' or from documents, the historian's experience as he works upon his material is different from that of the scientist. The coin or the manuscript is seen and touched, but the sense experience of handling a Roman *denarius* or of seeing the faded ink on a yellowing parchment is not the encounter which the historian is called upon to interpret. It is no more than a pathway to the experience. What is fundamental is the encounter of minds. It is, in Ranke's words, meeting 'the heroes face to face', though the hero may be only an obscure abbot trying to wangle a concession from the Pope. What the mind of the man in the past communicates to the mind of the historian is the essence of the experience.

As the scientist 'puts nature to the test', so the historian challenges the records of the past. A document must never be accepted at its face value, but must be cross questioned as rigorously as a witness in a law court. First it must be dated as accurately as possible by the style of its language, the type of material on which it is written or printed, the handwriting, the way it reflects the practices and conditions of a particular decade, and fits in with other documents of known date. The historian must then decide whether the document is genuine or a forgery, and if he accepts it as genuine he must still ask whether its contents may not be false, for ambassadors do not always tell the truth to kings, nor business agents to their employers. Even official documents tell lies. The *Rolls of Parliament*, at the point where they record the deposition of Richard II, are a biased compilation designed to justify his successor, Henry IV. Moreover, even an honest witness may have made a mistake or, being in a highly emotional state, may have failed to see and record the vital detail. Again he may have been so deeply involved in the situation he is describing that his narrative is coloured by his own hopes and fears.

There is a special problem here which does not trouble the scientist. Nature is mysterious and hides its secrets, but it does not tell lies. The evidence is truthful when you get it, though it may be hard to come by and harder still to interpret. But men do lie, either deliberately or unwittingly. There are no forgeries in nature; there are plenty in historical documents.

HISTORICAL NARRATIVE

When the historian has collected and sifted his evidence he has a tale to tell. He may contribute a highly technical argument to a learned journal, written with no more style than an average scientific paper in *Nature*, or he may write like a Macaulay or a Gibbon. His tale may be a detailed reconstruction of a single event, for example, the death of Hitler, made by piecing together many fragments of evidence. It may be a biography, the history of a village, the story of the economic fortunes of a particular industry, the development of political institutions, or of patterns of social change within a particular society.

There are, however, more complex forms of historical

writing. History may be written in the round. Here the historian is concerned with what Michelet described as 'the resurrection of life in its entirety', and the emphasis falls upon the last phrase: *la vie integrale*. Here the historian resurrects a total social situation as, for example, Jacob Burchardt did in *The Civilization of the Renaissance in Italy*, or as Professor R. W. Southern has done in *The Making of the Middle Ages*. In such books the conventional sub-divisions of political, economic, ecclesiastical and social history are ignored, and the life of the period as a complex yet unified whole is resurrected. This involves the use of one of the most subtle qualities of the historian, which has been called 'historical architecture' or 'span'. In such reconstructions the historian, like the architect, must see every detail in its proper relation to everything else. Every significant event and every characteristic of the period must be fitted into a pattern. It must be shown how that event led to this one, how that political trend interlocked with this economic or social characteristic, and how this relationship influenced the course of history. Moreover, the chief characters must be shown in the round, the statesmen not merely as politicians, the churchmen not merely as ecclesiastics. Marc Bloch wrote :

> Do you expect really to know the great merchant bankers of Renaissance Europe, vendors of cloth and spices, bankers of kings and the Emperor, by knowing their merchandise alone? Bear in mind that they were painted by Holbein, that they read Erasmus and Luther. To understand the attitude of the medieval vassal towards his seigneur you must inform yourself about his attitude to his God as well.[1]

The most complex type of historical writing endeavours to see the age-long story of the human race, in all centuries, in

[1] Quoted from Martin Wight, 'What Makes a Good Historian?' in *The Listener*, Feb. 17, 1955.

all civilizations, as a coherent whole; to uncover the directing forces of history, and to discern in this story a shape, a rhythm, and perhaps, a purpose.

Two outstanding examples of this kind of historical writing are Oswald Spengler's *The Decline of the West* and Arnold Toynbee's *A Study of History*. Spengler began by asking the question, 'Does world history present certain grand traits which must be traversed in an ordered obligatory sequence?' To this question he returned an affirmative answer. Great world events happen over and over again, following each other in the same order. There is a rhythm in history, a determined cycle of birth, maturity, age and death. To change the metaphor, human cultures have the same ordained pattern as nature; they have their springtime, high summer, autumn and winter. This cycle of every culture is inevitable and inescapable. The decay of a civilization is not a matter of human action and human frailty, but a doom, demonic and immense, which falls upon a culture in the late autumn and winter of its existence. We may be born on the golden summit of a ripe culture, or in the early winter of a decaying civilization. The choice is not ours.

Toynbee, like Spengler, is concerned with the rise and fall of civilizations, but his interpretation is not a rigid determinism. He seeks to find the reason for the genesis, the growth, the breakdown and the disintegration of the twenty-one civilizations and five 'arrested civilizations' which make up the recorded history of this earth. His clue for understanding the historical process is the concept of 'challenge and response'. Each civilization is confronted by a challenge, which in form will vary from place to place and from time to time. It may be the stimulus of hard, unfruitful land, or of new, unbroken country; of enemies from without, or of penalizations such as come upon an oppressed minority. In so far as the civilization or a group within it, responds to the challenge it will grow: at the moment when it fails any longer to respond it will begin to disintegrate. This is the rhythm but, in principle, it is not inevitable or inescapable. Whether a civilization responds to the challenge and grows, or refuses the challenge and disintegrates, depends upon the personal qualities of the men and women within it.

Professional historians, on the whole, reject these large-scale interpretations. Some flatly deny that history reveals any shape, rhythm or purpose. History is no more than a series of emergencies, and the crimes and sufferings of every age are enough to show that there is no rationality within it. Other historians take the view that it is impossible for men to discern the purpose in history, if purpose there be, because the whole canvas of human endeavour is too vast and too complex to be studied with the accuracy which their craft demands. The same facts can be arranged in many patterns, be seen from many perspectives and displayed in many lights. Standing at a particular point in time, himself involved in the historical process, with many gaps in his knowledge of the past, and ignorant of the future, the historian is in no position to offer us a unitary pattern embracing the whole of human experience. One might as well ask a snowflake on a glacier to consider the shape of the glacier, how it was formed and where it is going.

These are weighty arguments. Nevertheless there is an element in human experience which reacts passionately against the conclusion that the past is meaningless, and that the future will inevitably be one emergency following upon another. Sir Maurice Powicke once pointed out that 'the craving for an interpretation of history is so deep rooted that unless we have a constructive outlook over the past, we are drawn either to mysticism or to cynicism'.[1] The major difficulty is not so much the vast canvas and the complexity

[1] *Modern Historians and the Study of History* (1956), p. 174.

of detail, but rather that the historian has no standing ground outside history from which he can look down and survey the panorama of events as a single whole. By the diligent acquisition of knowledge, by the exercise of historical imagination, and by his skill in historical architecture, he can both enter sympathetically into the total situation of his chosen period and yet stand critically outside it; he can see a shape emerging from the details of those centuries. This is impossible for history as a whole unless we can find a vantage point from which we may look down and see the whole map of human experience spread out before us. In the last two chapters of this book I shall suggest, as an 'hypothesis', that just such a vantage point may be found by combining the insights of science, history and biblical religion.

HISTORICAL INTERPRETATION

Whether the historian publishes his results in a journal or writes a book he is faced by the problem of interpretation. Historical writing is never merely the setting down of a number of isolated facts; to a greater or lesser degree it is an attempt to say what the facts mean. If the events are not interpreted then the author is not writing history but compiling a chronicle.

The historian accumulates during his researches a great mass of material. When he plans his book he selects from this what seems important for his purpose. In part, of course, the selection is made for him because only a few of the events of the past have left any 'trace' or record. In principle everything that has ever happened is material for the historian: in practice, time and fortune have already sifted the evidence. Where a choice is possible he selects those characters, events, movements from which, in his judgment, significant consequences have developed. He then organizes his chosen material, giving it a certain shape and pattern, sometimes linking events in new sequences, high-lighting this fact or this character, putting the weight of emphasis here and not there.

This necessity for interpretation does not mean that good historical writing is bound to be partisan, twisting the evidence or suppressing awkward facts. Facts are sacred to the historian as to the scientist. But the nature of historical evidence demands an individual approach and a personal interpretation. A historian usually refuses today to set himself up as a judge of morals, but he must evaluate character, and concerning character there can always be more than one opinion. He must consider not merely human actions, but the inward springs which prompt action, and our judgment of another man's motives depends in part upon what we are ourselves. Thus each historian resurrects the past in his own way. He sees human behaviour through his own eyes and something of his own self is built into the story he tells. What he believes and values, what he approves of and judges worthless, as his trained eyes search the landscape of the past, will be an integral part of the history which he writes.

THE HISTORIAN'S EXPERIENCE

In a limited sense the phrase 'historical experience' refers to the *present* experience of the historian as he walks over a battlefield, visits a Norman church, handles a Greek or Roman coin, or sits in the Public Record Office examining a medieval charter. This experience is parallel to that of the scientist when he is out and about doing field research, or making calculations in his laboratory. The characteristic historical experience, however, occurs when the historian attempts to put himself back into the past, attaching himself to the men and women who lived in another century, in a different kind of world, seeing events through their eyes and emotions. Here the historian must be totally involved in the life of the past as an actor playing Hamlet must give himself in total commitment to the character.

The experience cannot, perhaps, be realized in all its fullness. 'The historian', wrote Professor Herbert Butterfield, 'can never quite know men from the inside . . . never quite carry his enquiries to that innermost region where the final play of motive and the point of responsibility can be decided.' Yet the experience can be entered into by the use of imaginative sympathy. Professor Butterfield used as an example the massacre of St Bartholomew's Day. The first task is to establish the whole range of facts and conditioning circumstances, and to discover Catherine de' Medici's views, intentions, motives, and the range of options open to her at the decisive moment. Then :

> We are called to resurrect the whole occasion, and to see with Catherine, feel with her, hold our breath with her, and meet the future with all her apprehension. If by imaginative sympathy we can put ourselves in her place in this way, not only envisaging the situation in all its detail, but apprehending it in all its vividness and intensity until we reach the point at which we could almost conceive ourselves making the drastic decision, or at least have a sense of just what it would take to carry us across the border to such a decision—then we are historians indeed.[1]

From the writings of present-day historians who have entered fully into this kind of experience we may cite Miss C. V. Wedgwood's study of the reign of King Charles I in the years immediately prior to the outbreak of the Civil War.[2] The book is firmly based upon the great mass of evidence available to an historian working on the seventeenth century : on the State Papers, the Strafford Manuscripts, the Journals of both Houses of Parliament, as well

---

[1] *History and Human Relations* (1951), pp. 116, 124.
[2] *The King's Peace 1637-1641* (1955), pp. 426-7.

as upon many other documents. All this material, however, will not of itself engender historical experience. It must be interpreted by the historian's controlled use of the imagination. In the following extract Miss Wedgwood recaptures the experience of King Charles on Sunday, May 9, 1641, as he sat in a room in his palace at Whitehall, confronted by the Bill of Attainder, demanding the death of his chief servant, Lord Strafford, sent up to him by both Houses of Parliament.

In painful anxiety the King sent for the judges to advise him on the state of the law in Strafford's case. When they had gone his doubts were still unresolved. He sought spiritual guidance. How could he consent to the Bill when it was against his conscience to do so? Strafford's letter might release him from an obligation to Strafford : it did not release him from an obligation to God. On this point and no other he called in those in whose spiritual gifts he trusted. He sent for the Primate of Ireland, Archbishop Ussher, then on a visit to London. Ussher, who received the message in the pulpit of St Paul's, Covent Garden, sent to say that he could wait on His Majesty only when he had done his duty to God. It was the kind of answer which pleased Charles. But Ussher, when he arrived later in the day, gave it as his opinion categorically that the King should in no circumstances perform an act against his conscience. William Juxton, Bishop of London, resolved the moral problem in the same way and with the same firmness.

Bishop Williams spoke round and about in a very different fashion. He pointed out to the King the evils that might ensue from his refusal to gratify his people. He discoursed learnedly of the dual character of kingship, showing how the King, as a private man, may think and act in one way, but, as a King, is bound to think and act differently. The King in his private conscience could not condemn Strafford, but what of the King's public conscience? Could he load it with the fearful responsibility of bloodshed? He must go against the dictates of conscience either as a man or as a King, whichever decision he took; as a King, was he not more answerable than as a man to God from whom his power came? The argument was subtle and well urged. It moved the King. What had been a crime against his conscience appeared to him in a new light—as a duty: with tears in his eyes he gave his consent to the Bill of Attainder. 'My Lord of Strafford's condition', he said, 'is happier than mine.'

In such a manner, 'living through everything again', the historian sets out to recapture the inward life of the past. He needs attachment in order that he may get close to people, and also justice that he may withdraw a little and, like a wise arbitrator, report fairly each point of view. His bed-rock experience, unlike that of the scientist, is not of things or of events, but of persons. What he strives for is an 'I-Thou' relationship with the men and women of the past. In this attachment to the thoughts and feelings of other men the historian reaches down to the roots of things. The 'tracks' and 'traces' of a bygone civilization, the official State Papers, the partisan chronicles, the private diaries, make up a revelation. They are the self-disclosure of historical characters to the historian. He receives the revelation and makes what he can of it according to his own personality and powers. He may make little of it, or much. But the revelation is given. Men and women, long since dead, speak to those who live.

4

THE RELIGIOUS EXPERIENCE
OF MAN

THE Gifford Lectures delivered by William James in 1904, and published under the title *The Varieties of Religious Experience*, have been regarded for more than half a century as a standard work on the subject. They are, however, misleading and perverse because the total impression left upon the reader is that religion must be a very odd affair, and religious experience, in all its varieties, a most peculiar experience. William James appears to have been aware of this criticism because in the preface he half apologizes for 'the convulsions of piety' which seem to offer 'a caricature of the subject'. The book begins with a chapter on 'Religion and Neurology': there are further chapters on 'The Religion of Healthy-mindedness' (which includes a study of the 'mind-cure' movement); on 'The Sick Soul', 'The Divided Self', 'Saintliness' and 'Mysticism'. The precise meaning of these titles is, of course, carefully defined in the text, but none the less (and in spite of the author's disclaimer) religious experience is here represented as a strange phenomenon almost entirely divorced from the basic experiences of a man's life. We need not deny the reality of such unusual encounters. Something happened, no doubt, to the men and women whom William James called in evidence. They often reveal abnormal psychological states: that they throw any light upon the essential characteristics of religious experience is highly doubtful.

When William James described religious experience in these terms he was merely pushing one stage further a long tradition of Christian apologists. When Protestants write or speak on the subject they are all too liable to quote St Paul's encounter on the road to Damascus, or the moment when John Wesley felt his heart strangely warmed in a house in Aldersgate Street. Catholic writers favour St John of the Cross or St Theresa of Avila or, on a more popular level, St Bernadette of Lourdes. That something happened to these men and women need not be denied, provided that the historical evidence satisfies us, but to lean heavily upon their experiences, and to use them as arguments, is to distort the nature of religious experience.

The experience of the religious man is, basically, *everyday experience*. It is our common encounter with men and with things. Thus it differs from scientific and historical experience which, in their fullness, are the outcome of particular interests and specialized training. Religious men are not usually experts in certain fields, such as natural science or history, though simply as men they enter both. Such technical knowledge as they possess is normally limited and acquired at second hand. Their experience is diffuse and infinitely varied, and it is difficult to impose order upon it because, in principle, it embraces every encounter which may confront a human being. Because the religious man is a man, things happen to him. Because he is a man he climbs over and passes through barriers in search of experience. He is endowed with the five senses; his environment is the natural world which scientists explore, and his inheritance is the past which historians resurrect. He lives, as do all men, in a network of human relationships and is, in himself, an amalgam of body, intellect, emotion, imagination and spirit. There is only one human consciousness—not a special sort of scientists, another for historians and a third sort for saints.

Religious men do not inhabit a different world from that of other men, and often they interpret our common experiences as others do. But they extend the range of the interpretation, probing the experience in a different direction, seeking to uncover a reality which gives unity and meaning to nature, to man and to his past. Experience is like a great marble block on which many sculptors are at work. The religious man, like the scientist and the historian, has his own point of entry, and drives in his chisel at a particular angle. This, of course, is not to claim that the religious interpretation of experience is always right or always profound. It is sometimes in error where the scientific interpretation is correct; sometimes superficial where the historical judgment is realistic and rich in meaning. Religious men are not protected from error in their interpretation of experience. What distinguishes them from others is their conviction that their particular point of entry into the marble block will reveal a unique and indispensable aspect of reality.

The religious man, as he treads the common paths of life, is deliberately seeking an encounter with God. As the scientist searches for experiences which may disclose to him a new fragment of truth concerning the natural world; as the historian cultivates those experiences which bring him nearer to the essential quality of the past; so the religious man treasures those encounters which may bring him nearer to the reality which gives a new depth of meaning to all experience.

The religious man seeks an encounter with God, but to ask 'Where is God?' is to pose the wrong question. Inevitably it localizes God. Even to give the most comprehensive of the orthodox answers and to say that God is 'omnipresent' suggests that God, like a material body, has mass, velocity and extension in space. The more profitable question is to ask, 'In what kinds of human situation, in what types of experience, may a man encounter God?' In principle, any situation, whether exalted or commonplace, may lead to an understanding of, and confidence in, God. Science takes the whole world of experience as its province: there can be a history of anything. Religion also claims the whole world of experience for itself.

It is this comprehensiveness which makes it difficult to impose any pattern upon religious experience or to discuss it in an orderly fashion, and to find for it a conceptual scheme. Nevertheless, the attempt must be made. In the following pages five basic experiences are examined, all of which are, in principle, universal. Every man is capable of receiving them. They are highly significant encounters which we may call 'pattern experiences', or 'paradigmatic experiences', using a phrase coined by the late Karl Mann-heim.[1] They are: (1) the experience of the natural world, (2) the inheritance of the past, (3) the search for integrity, (4) the encounter with other persons, (5) the experience of existence. Each of these has, as we shall see, a positive and a negative aspect. When we encounter the positive side of the experience it calls for our joyous affirmation. When we encounter the negative side there is a challenge to live through, and to come to terms with, helplessness, frustration and despair. What seems to hold these five experiences together in a conceptual scheme is not only their universality, but also the possibility that in each of them, when we penetrate deeply enough, we seem to come to the roots of things.

[1] *Diagnosis of Our Time* (1943), p. 134: 'The religious focus is a way of interpreting life from the centre of some paradigmatic experience.'

1. *The natural world*

Our common experience of nature is, of course, universal, though it comes to the city dweller with greatly diminished power. Where once, in rural societies, it was sharp, insistent and continuous, now to the tenants of flats and bed-sitting rooms it is intermittent, sought for at weekends and on holidays, or largely ignored. But none can wholly escape its impact, for nature is the air we breathe, the water we drink, the light by which we see, the force of gravity which anchors us to the earth. It is the context of our living.

It is the task of the scientist to explore the natural world, but as a scientist his experience of nature is limited and confined by the method of abstraction and analysis which he so frequently employs. The method is indeed a master tool for specific purposes. The scientist in much of his research turns away from any attempt to see a phenomenon in the round; to experience it in its manifold variety, and seizes rather upon one or two properties, dissociates them from all other properties, and concentrates observation, experiment and measurement upon them.

By this method a distinction is made between the primary and secondary qualities of an object. A feather, to use Galileo's example, has (we say) colour, lustre, beauty, but these are secondary qualities. They cannot be measured on a scale or tested by experiment. They may only exist in the mind and in the imagination of the observer and they are, perhaps, illusory. The feather also has primary qualities : shape, size, quantity, motion, and it is these measurable properties which the scientist abstracts and studies. Thus Newton when he reflected upon the problem of the falling apple ignored its colour, taste and roundness, and abstracted the one property of motion.[1]

The ordinary man, on the other hand, looks upon a natural scene as a whole. This is experience in the round. He sees a feather fall from a swan's neck and float in the water. He is aware of its shape and size and of its slow motion on the water's surface; aware too of its soft whiteness, its fragile brightness and its delicate beauty. But his eye embraces not only the feather but the swan with its proudly arched neck and serene progress; not only the swan but the lake fringed with reeds; not only the lake but the landscape of fields, woods and distant hills.

The scientist is concerned with repeatable events in nature. Everyone, of course, has experience of this—the rising and setting of the sun, the delphinium flower springing from the delphinium seed. But we also possess a sense of 'something special' about even the continually repeated events of nature. They are

> like events, never from world's beginning to world's end the same event. Each leaf of oak and ash and thorn is a unique embodiment of the pattern, and for some this very year may be *the* embodiment, the first ever seen and recognized, though oaks have put forth leaves for countless generations of men.[2]

There is in such experiences an emotional content quite out of place in a science laboratory or a research station. There is enjoyment, a recognition of beauty, a sense of tranquillity. A man takes pleasure in a country walk, loves his garden, longs for a sight of the sea, seeks solitude in the mountains, feels an urge to meet the challenge of the north face of the Eiger. On the other hand—and this is the nega-

[1] There are aspects of scientific thought and practice in which this method is transcended, and an attempt is made to see nature as a whole. See chapter 7.

[2] J. R. R. Tolkien, *Tree and Leaf* (1964), p. 51.

tive side of the experience—he is appalled by what he calls 'the cruelty of nature'; the savage struggle for existence, the uncontrollable fury of earthquake and hurricane. Entering into this more fully rounded and, in part, emotional experience, he makes value judgments which are wholly unscientific.

To the scientist it is a function of wheat, oats and barley to produce seed as the end product of the natural cycle of growth, but to a hungry man bread is a necessity. To the scientist water is the normal oxide of hydrogen, but to a thirsty man it is a benediction. To a geologist, the Pennine hills are composed of carboniferous limestone and Millstone Grit, but to the factory workers of Sheffield or Leeds they are places of beauty and refreshment. To the meteorologist a cyclone is a particular type of storm characterized by high winds rotating about a calm centre of low atmospheric pressure, but to those whose homes stand in its path it is an irrational visitation, a savage assault upon a pleasant land; a killer, derisive of man's life and property. Aldous Huxley in an early essay entitled *Wordsworth in the Tropics* wrote that :

> wandering in the hothouse of the jungle, he (Wordsworth) would not have felt so serenely certain of those 'Presences of Nature', those 'Souls of Lonely Places' which he was in the habit of worshipping on the shores of Windermere and Rydal. The sparse inhabitants of the equatorial forest are all believers in devils. When one has visited, in even the most superficial manner, the places where they live, it is difficult not to share their faith. The jungle is marvellous, fantastic, beautiful; but it is also terrifying, it is also profoundly sinister.[1]

There is, as we can see, a rhythm in our natural environment, an interlocking of innumerable processes to produce the harvest; there is the changing beauty of the seasons, and also the hazards which threaten our lives. Nature goes on

[1] *Rotunda (Selected Works, 1932)*, p. 873.

its way, fulfilling its proper function without reference to what men want. It is both an abundant treasury of gifts and a dangerous threat. Yet it is our home and without it we could not survive.

This brings us back to a deeper aspect of the negative side of the experience. The hungry man may not find bread, nor the thirsty man water. The mountaineer may slip on the north face of the Eiger, the man in the path of the hurricane may be hurled down. Then, as we say, they stand between life and death. At one moment the man exists: he is. In the next moment—unless help comes—he will not exist: he will not be. In that moment of time he is confronted by the shock of non-being. He has come to the abyss of nothingness and stands at its very edge.

2. *A sense of the past*

Each of us has a personal ancestry. Behind us lies a long line of men and women which stretches back to the first *Homo sapiens,* and then further back still to our animal ancestry. As individuals we are what we are largely because of our personal inheritance. Each of us, likewise, lives in a community which has deep roots in the past. Even a new emergent nation like Ghana or Kenya is largely what it is because of its past history of tribalism on the one hand and colonialism on the other.

Many conscious attitudes are possible towards our distant past. The most dominant in present-day society appears to be one of indifference or even rejection. In art, in literature, in morals, in politics, in religion, tradition is regarded as an encumbrance, the past a brake upon progress. Technology, we feel, has created for us a totally new kind of civilization, and in so doing has engineered a complete break with our inheritance. Such an attitude, however, is a refusal of experience. Nothing can alter the fact that we have a personal ancestry and are members of a community with roots in the past. To recognize this is to possess a certain sense of security. So a man may travel a long distance to visit the village where his grand-parents were born, or take a lively interest in local history or archeology. By strengthening our links with the past we seem to increase our feeling of stability. We know, of course, that life for our ancestors was not really stable. Yet by looking back we can see how events worked themselves out. We can see the unpredictable consequences, the way in which happenings which seemed meaningless when they occurred, fit together into some sort of pattern. In short this security is ours when we can see our personal history and the history of our world in the round.

Such a sense of security, however, usually arises from our experience of distant history. It is the time span which gives us a sense of permanence. Our experience of the events which we have lived through ourselves is often the negative side of historical experience. Here there seems to be no hint of a pattern or meaning. Here there is no security but only uncertainty, because the consequences of the events have hardly begun to work themselves out. Here is anxiety, horror and fear, because the shadow of that first atomic bomb has spread into a vast cloud overshadowing all we think or do. Here is bewilderment, because to live in a technological society demands fresh social patterns, unfamiliar reactions in a new kind of environment. Here is doubt, because the political history of the past fifty years and the new scientific knowledge have played havoc with traditional politics, ethics and theology. Yet there are always men, like the great prophets of Israel, who live through the darkest days of uncertainty, anxiety and fear, confident that even this negative side of historical experience is a necessary part of the pattern, and holds a meaning within itself.

We have already seen that Christianity is a 'religion of

historians'. Both the Old and the New Testaments consist largely of historical documents, and the centre of the Christian faith is not in a theological statement but in the life history of Jesus of Nazareth. Christians, therefore, have a particular incentive to seek historical experience. There are, indeed, New Testament scholars who, despairing of any historical encounter in the Gospels, argue that the events of the life of Jesus are, in any case, irrelevant to Christianity. It is the faith of the Church (apparently whether or not that faith is historically grounded) which must be the Christian's starting point and standing ground. 'To understand Jesus all that is necessary is to proclaim that he has come.'[1] This highly debatable position certainly does not reflect the experience of ordinary men. They do find an encounter with history both in the Gospels and in the practice of the Christian life. The great majority, no doubt, have never been able to attain to that characteristic historical experience of 'living through everything again', recapturing the essential quality of Jesus and his disciples as St Francis did, or as Albert Schweitzer has done in a very different fashion. Yet they do possess an historical experience of their religion. Often it has been stimulated through Christian art and architecture; through visits to ancient cathedrals and abbeys which mirror a past way of Christian life; through the stained glass of Chartres and York, the statues, carvings and altar paintings of great masters (as well as through abominable mass-produced statuettes and pictures). Through the eye and the ear they have sought, like the historian Ranke, 'to meet the heroes face to face'. And the experience has been given through Christian worship, through familiarity with the biblical narrative and through a personal commitment to Jesus. Many a Christian can make his own the words of St Bernard of Clairvaux :

[1] E. Brunner in *Kerygma and Myth*, vol. i (1953), p. 117.

When I name Jesus I recall to myself a man gentle and lowly in heart, kind, temperate, pure, pitiful, marked by every grace and holiness; a man too who is almighty God, who heals me by His example and fortifies me by His aid . . . So I take my examples from his manhood and my assistance from His power.[1]

3. *The search for integrity*

There is in most men, at least in a partly developed form, an inner restlessness until their manifold experiences fit together into some kind of pattern. A man's personal life is more than an assortment of different threads; it is a web of knowledge and experience, and if the web is broken he loses his sense of harmony and completeness. Thought and action become a series of desperate expedients.

One aspect of this desire for integrity is the scholar's passion to dig down to the very heart of his particular subject; to examine critically all the evidence, to establish the facts with precision, and to interpret correctly the relationship between them. To leave one detail unchecked, one piece of data unaccounted for, would be to deny his own standards. This, however, is not the ideal of scholars alone. It is found also in the pride of a mechanic to understand perfectly his machine, of a mountaineer to master his craft, of a musician to be completely in tune with his instrument.

There is a moral aspect of the search for integrity in the desire to find some principle for living. It is, of course, common enough to take life as it comes, but if a man grows dissatisfied with this hand-to-mouth moral existence he may turn to the discipline of a rigid moral code, or seek for an ethical formula which he can wholeheartedly accept, such as 'being true to oneself', 'loving one's neighbour', or 'respecting the personality of others'. Whatever principle he selects,

[1] Quoted from G. L. Prestige, *Fathers and Heretics* (1940), p. 386.

he is looking for a loom and a shuttle which will weave his thoughts and actions into an harmonious pattern.

The negative side of this experience is, in the first place, the failure to find any resting place for the mind, or any guidance for living. This is total doubt, where the spirit of enquiry, even the desire to know, disappears. And there is a second aspect: the failure to face up to the demands of the truth a man has made his own; to carry through the principle for living which he has accepted. This is the experience of guilt—the betrayal of oneself. When these things happen, when a man experiences total doubt or deep-seated guilt, life begins to disintegrate unless he can find a way back to a life of integrity. He no longer tries to think his way through his situation, but takes refuge in stubborn prejudice. He reacts to a moral challenge, not by making a judgment, but by drifting with the tide. Then he is a stranger; a lost man in an alien world.

4. *The encounter with other persons*

The field of religion is the field of personal experience. The centre of this field is the experience we have of other persons in relation to ourselves. In all our relations with one another we are in the field of religion, and since there is nothing in the whole range of our experience which may not be seen or valued in its bearings upon our relations with one another, there is nothing at all which does not belong, directly or indirectly, to the field of religion.[1]

Professor John Macmurray's position, as in this quotation, is the primacy of the personal. His aim is to develop a concept of the personal in which both the inorganic and the organic can be included. Yet it is difficult to see how everything in our experience is connected, even indirectly, with other persons. Indeed, on p. 23 of the same book, Macmurray

[1] J. Macmurray, *The Structure of Religious Experience* (1946), p. 45.

wrote that 'the velocity with which a body falls to the earth lies very near the centre of interest for science', and it would be hard indeed to relate this scientific phenomenon in any significant way to our personal relationships. Nevertheless, the encounter with other persons is a 'paradigmatic experience'. It can be a pathway to God and, for some men and women, it may be the very point of encounter with God.

This has been argued persuasively by Mr John Wren-Lewis:

> In the moments when we do see the universe as it really is we encounter a profound mystery which is the clue to the meaning of the word 'God'. Our common speech gives away this mystery: we speak of falling *in* love, of love being 'bigger than both of us'; we say that 'love will find a way' . . . Our very being as persons, in fact, comes from our encounters with each other—and since this is true for each of us then there must really be something between us which is there before us, and is bigger than all of us. Here, in fact, at the heart of personal life, we have an actual experience of creation—not just an idea of the Universe being made by somebody, but direct knowledge of ourselves being created by a power 'between man and man'. It is this knowledge, I believe, upon which all religion is grounded, the knowledge which St John summed up when he said, 'God is love'. It is from this point, and from this point alone, that our understanding of religion can begin.[1]

This statement is founded upon a widespread and deeply felt experience, but like the argument of Professor Macmurray it claims too much. It is wrong to narrow down the situations of the divine encounter to a single point, and to say that 'it is from this point, and this point alone, that our understanding of religion can begin'. Experience is shaped like a tree not like a telegraph pole. To stare at one branch, ignoring the tree as a whole, is to miss its meaning and its

[1] *Return to the Roots: a Study of the Meaning of the word God* p. 10.

wonder. It is the scientific method of abstraction applied at the wrong point. Moreover, if there is but a single point of encounter then religion is an exclusive thing. Miss this particular experience and religion is meaningless. Yet there are scholars for whom the very heart of a life-time's experience is not 'falling in love' but the search for truth. There are painters, musicians, dancers whose art is their true centre. There are those who have not known the 'actual experience of creation', for love has never come to them.

It has become something of a fashion in these days to base the argument for religion exclusively upon our experience of personal relationships. The argument, as it is usually stated, all too easily ignores the negative side of the experience. 'Hell—that is other people,' said Sartre in a famous phrase. There is a kind of loving which feeds on power and which becomes cruelly possessive. There are personal relationships of scorn and hate. This, of course, is not to deny that the experience of giving and receiving love, and even of giving love where it is not valued or returned, is one of our 'paradigmatic' experiences. At the heart of it is a mystery which is none the less a revelation. It is an encounter which points beyond itself.

5. The experience of existence

This, though it may be unrecognized, is our universal and omnipresent experience. Whenever 'something happens' to us we run up against existence; whenever we go through, or seek to climb over, barriers in search of experience we are seeking the primary encounter contained in the words: I am, he is, things are.

This experience is the source of wonder without which religion dies, but it is not the wonder which impels the scientist and the historian in their researches. The behaviour of the fundamental particles or the motion of the stars in the sky set the physicist or the astronomer wondering 'how?' and 'why?' The behaviour of men and women in the past prompts the historian to wonder 'how?' and 'why?', and to search for an explanation. The source of religious wonder is that particles and stars, men and women, exist at all. Such a realization of being sets the religious man wondering 'at' a mystery which will not one day be solved. The mystery is that things are. 'Not how the world is, is the mystical, but that it is,'[1] wrote Wittgenstein, and Paul Tillich has pointed to 'the astonishing pre-rational fact that there is something and not nothing'.[2] The most significant thing, for example, that a man can say about a tree is not that it is beautiful, or that it is useful for making cradles, marriage beds and coffins, but that *it is*. The most profound thing that a man can say about himself is simply *I am*.

When I affirm my existence by speaking the words, 'I am', I assert myself as an individual separated from all others, with an inner personal centre and freedom of action, even though the limits of my freedom are confined. I assert my existence, but I do more than this. I assert that my existence has meaning; that I am able to recognize good from evil, that I share in the creative spirit of man. To affirm my own existence, to affirm the existence of the universe, is to rejoice in, to shout aloud for, the positives in life, even in the face of life's negatives. For there is a negative side to this omnipresent experience. There are moments, usually rare in life, but universal as we approach death, when we are aware of the threat of non-being. We know that we are coming to the edge of the abyss of nothingness. And, even in the midst of life, there are barren periods when to affirm one's being

[1] *Tractatus logico-philosophicus* (No. 644). Quoted from F. C. Copleston, *Aquinas* (Pelican ed., 1955), p. 65.
[2] *The Courage to Be* (Fontana ed., 1962), p. 48. Readers of Tillich will be aware of my debt to him in this section.

appears to be a mocking absurdity, because life is meaningless in our eyes. There are times of bitter frustration when we wish that we were not.

> Why is light given to him that is in misery,
> and life to the bitter in soul,
> who long for death, but it comes not
> and dig for it more than for hid treasures? (*Job* 3.20-21).

Yet 'I am' is a proud thing to say.

AT THE ROOTS OF THINGS

These five 'pattern experiences', when they are entered into and lived through in depth, have one characteristic in common. They all have an elemental quality. We are aware in these encounters that we have come up against that which cannot be evaded or overcome. There is a resistance; a limitation is imposed upon us. Yet frustration comes only if we do not recognize that here we have come to the roots of things. If we know what it is that confronts us, then there is a sense of liberation. We can be in harmony; we can co-operate. The experience can be one of joyful affirmation.

The American atomic scientist, J. Robert Oppenheimer, discussing whether when we find something in science, we 'invent' or 'discover' it, has written:

> We are, of course, free in our tradition and in our practice, and to a much more limited extent, individually, to decide where to look at nature, how to look at nature, what questions to put, with what instruments and with what purpose. But we are not in the least bit free to settle what we find. Man must certainly be free to invent the idea of mass, as Newton did, and as it has been refined and redefined, but having done so, we have not been free to find that the mass of the light quantum or the neutrino is anything but zero. We are free in the start of things. We are free as to how to go about it; but then the rock of what the world is shapes this freedom with a necessary answer.[1]

[1] *Encounter*, October 1962, pp. 8-9.

C

It is not only in nature that we come up against this 'rock of what the world is'. None of us can evade the elemental fact that we dwell in space and time, that our personal history, our ancestry is what it is, that the communities in which we dwell and which shape our lives, come out of an unalterable past. And the history we have lived through and helped to make, is what it is. The atom bomb has been invented and the 'know-how' will never be forgotten. It has been dropped and we are not free to find it anything but a perpetual threat to our peace of mind. The technological revolution has come to transform our ways of living. We can no more repudiate its effects than we can repudiate the consequences, in Britain and northern Europe, of the sixteenth century Reformation. In history facts are what they are.

In our more intimate personal experiences there is this same encounter with 'the rock of what the world is'. The integrity of the scientist and the historian is seen in their reverence for fact. The one does not demand freedom to make the mass of the light quantum anything but zero : the other will not fail to check and recheck the facts on which his reconstruction of past events stands or falls. Integrity is the still point of their turning world, and in this moral quality they come to the roots of things. What is true here for the professional scholar is true also in common experience. If we succeed in finding a resting place for the mind and a principle for living, we know that there is something elemental in the truth we embrace; something obligatory in the principle we have freely accepted. The essence of this experience is that we have reached bedrock, though the area of the rock may be small and its surface precarious. Here, too, we know that our freedom is shaped by a necessary answer.

In our personal relationships, and especially in the relationship of love, we come up against the other who cannot be overcome or evaded. As soon as we seek to ignore the other, or to impose our will upon him, we move out of the realm of truly personal relationships. When we reach the depths of this experience we have no desire to overcome or to evade the other, only the desire to unite, to co-operate, to affirm the relationship. For the other must be encouraged to say of himself, 'I am', and of us, 'He is'.

The experience of existence is indeed the clue to understanding all our 'paradigmatic experiences' in depth. Here we are at the roots of things. Is this the end of the search? Have we here reached finality, or is the experience of 'the rock of what the world is' one that in itself demands interpretation?

The deep division between Humanists and Theists occurs precisely at this point. Humanists, of course, are as varied in their convictions as any other group of people. Many of them, I think, would accept the general argument from experience, though with reservations about some points in it. But here is the end of the road for them. They have come, as it were, to a great mountain wall and the pass climbing up from the valley goes no further. Here they may continue to ask 'how?' and 'why?'. Here they may sit in the sunshine, or weather the storms, wondering at the elemental quality of the mountain wall. For them this is the riddle in which we must rest. The pass goes no further.

For Theists there is a track which leads still further into the heart of the mountain. Even the elemental experience itself, they believe, needs to be interpreted, because there is no reason for saying that the universe confers existence upon itself. Our pattern experiences are not invented but given, and it would be meaningless folly for a man to say to himself, 'I will be'. So the track leads to Being-Itself, to God the ground of all existence.

There is no possible way of proving by logical argument

that the track exists and that at the end of it we encounter Being-Itself. To move from our 'pattern experiences' to God is a deliberate, freely chosen act of faith, resembling that other act of faith which we all make when we move from our sense experiences to belief in an objective universe. These two 'pre-rational judgments' are not parallel cases, but they have this important similarity. In both, clues which lie within our common experience are used to organize and give final coherence to the totality of experience. You cannot make sense of the experience of seeing without believing that there is something to see, and equally you cannot do full justice to the total experience of existing without believing in the Ground of Being.

The Christian, however, takes one final step. Out of these 'pattern experiences' his faith is born, and it is faith not simply in Being-Itself, but in 'Being-Itself-as-gracious'.[1] To ask merely, 'Does God exist?', even if we return an affirmative answer, explains very little about the depth of our experiences. To believe in God as gracious, which implies that God and man are linked in a living relationship, is the clue to understanding all the positive elements in our encounters with nature, history, the desire for integrity, personal relationships, and our own existence in an existing universe.

Yet, as we have seen, there is a negative side to all these experiences. We cannot shrug off what we describe as 'the indifference and downright cruelty in nature', or the crimes and follies of history, or the failure to maintain our integrity, or the collapse of love, or the fact of death, in order to maintain our belief that God is gracious. The second part of this book deals with our experience of pattern and relationship, and this may throw some indirect light upon the

[1] See John Macquarrie, 'How is Theology Possible?' in *The Honest to God Debate*, ed. D. L. Edwards (1963), p. 188.

problem of evil and the problem of pain. One thing may be said as we come to the end of this description of the religious man's experience. No argument can offer a satisfying answer or bring comfort to those who suffer. The answer and the comfort, if they are possible at all, come out of that elemental experience of which I have written. We come up against that which cannot be evaded or overcome, and yet there is a sense of being sustained, of not being allowed to fall into utter despair or complete non-being. The darkness, we find, is light enough. It was this experience of which Gerard Manley Hopkins wrote :

> Thou mastering me
> God ! giver of breath and bread;
> World's strand, sway of the sea;
>   Lord of living and dead;
> Thou hast bound bones and veins in me, fastened me flesh,
> And after it almost unmade me, what with dread,
>   Thy doing; and dost thou touch me afresh?
> Over again I feel thy finger and find thee.[1]

[1] *The Wreck of the Deutschland*, stanza 1.

5

THE DOUBLE STATUS OF MAN

I N the first part of this book the characteristic experiences of the scientist, the historian and the man of religion have been examined in some detail, and the argument has been that the deeper these experiences are explored the closer they come together. In this second part the same argument is pursued in a somewhat different direction. There are connecting rods in our experience which link together the worlds of science, history and Christianity. This does not mean that there are separate and distinct experiences which more or less resemble each other, but rather that there are bedrock experiences, common to us all, which appear in different forms according to the activities which we pursue. Two examples are discussed at length. The first is man's double status in the universe, and the second is his search for a pattern which will unite his manifold experiences into a balanced and harmonious whole.

Whether a man's central concern is with nature, with history or with religion, he discovers at the roots of things that his relationship with the universe is subtle and complex. Here, as we have seen, he knows himself to be free and yet bound. He is self-reliant, intrepidly creative, changing the world, shaping his institutions, and yet he must bow to necessity. His relationship, however, is still more complex. In a unique way he is a participant in the universe which he studies and explores, and often transforms. In seeking experience he discovers that he is himself part of the source of experience. In pursuing knowledge he is not only the pursuer, but also the pursued. He is the traveller, but also the pathway. This is his double status in the universe.

THE SCIENTIST AS PARTICIPANT

It used to be held (and no doubt is still believed by many) that a scientist is an independent and unbiassed observer of something which he calls nature, which is clearly and at all points other than himself. He stands (so it was supposed) over against nature, wholly apart from it as a subject studying an object. In fact the status of the scientist is far more complex than is suggested by the traditional picture of an astronomer peering through a telescope at a distant star, or a biologist observing a specimen under a microscope. The scientist is himself part of nature which his instruments are designed to explore; part of the pattern of relationships which his mind sees. An observer of nature, he is also a fragment of what he observes. He maps the orbits of the planets, measures their speed and their density, and can predict where any star will be in the sky at any given moment, yet, like the stars, he too possesses mass, velocity and extension in space. He studies the constitution of proteins and the metabolism of living organisms, but he also is physics and chemistry, and the elements of his physical make-up are the fundamental particles. He studies man's natural environment, but is himself part of it. He is an observer, but always a significant factor in what he observes. Seeking to interpret experiences which come to him from without, he finds that he is an integral part of the source of that experience; discovering or creating patterns in nature, he is himself part of the pattern.

I am a thing in space. With my hand I can touch my eye; with my eye I can see my hand. I am object. But I am not only the eye that is seen and the hand that is touched. I am also the eye that sees, the hand that touches.[1]

We are a long way from Bacon's natural philosopher, 'consulting only things themselves'.[2] When William Harvey discovered the circulation of the blood in 1628 he consulted things themselves. He made thorough anatomical studies of reptiles and mammals, but he was also, at the central point of his research, consulting himself. William Harvey, in fact, encountered William Harvey.

Two epoch-making scientific theories have brought this complex relationship into strong relief. The first is the theory of evolution. The more restricted meaning of this term refers to the biological theory that more recent organisms evolve from earlier ones by slight favourable variations, brought about by natural selection. The word 'evolution' is used here in a wider sense to denote the development in time of a vast and intricate pattern linking together in firm relationships every part of our environment from the oldest star to that latest newcomer upon the earth, *Homo sapiens*. It is when the scientific observer realizes that he is one shaped piece in the pattern which he seeks to put together that his double status is revealed to him. Those who study the processes of evolution are writing their own autobiographies, and those who philosophize about these processes are considering not only their own ancestry but, more significantly, their own place in the whole pattern. The discovery that man fits into the evolutionary process, a fact which in the middle years of the nineteenth century provoked such violent controversy between geologists and biologists on the one hand, and some sections of orthodox Christianity on the other, has now, by a strange turn of the wheel, discredited the simple picture of the man of science, objective where others are enmeshed in

[1] C. F. von Weizsäcker, *The History of Nature* (1931), p. 10.
[2] Preface to *De Augmentis*, p. 16.

subjectivism, standing apart and disengaged, where others are lured from the straight and narrow path of truth by involvement in their environment. Physicists and naturalists must now realize, wrote Pierre Teilhard de Chardin, that

> they are committed body and soul to the network of relationships they thought to cast upon things from outside: in fact they are caught in their own net . . . Object and subject marry and mutually transform each other in the act of knowledge, and from now on man willy-nilly finds his own image stamped on all he looks at.[1]

There is a distinction to be made at this point. The scientist is part of the world he studies, but this does not mean in all instances that 'object and subject marry and mutually transform each other'. William Harvey encountered William Harvey, but this did not affect in any way the accuracy and completeness of his discovery. On the other hand, there are instances where the scientist's involvement does alter what he is observing. The impossibility of measuring simultaneously both the velocity and the position of a particle is a case in point. To see where the particle was, you have to make it go elsewhere. The work of the sociologist, with its inevitable interaction of observer and observed, is another example.

There is a third and more subtle situation which reveals the scientist's double status, though in a different way. One consequence of Einstein's concept of relativity is that man's observations, experiments, measurements and interpretations are seen to depend upon where he happens to be in the vast complex which we call nature. Most day-to-day scientific observations are made from a point on the surface of the earth, but with the successful launching of space satellites there are now other observation posts located elsewhere in the universe. If we free our thoughts from this planet which

[1] *The Phenomenon of Man* (1959), p. 32.

is our familiar home, scientific knowledge is seen in a new light.

Even observations from the earth are made from a tiny speck of matter in motion in its own orbit round the sun. When we observe the stars we are observing other specks of matter, some larger, some smaller than our own, travelling at their own individual speeds and in their own orbits. The observer is in motion; what he observes is also in motion, and the speeds and directions are different.

A simple illustration of the consequences of this can be given. Consider the measurement of the speed of a railway train. If the observer with his stop-watches is standing at a stationary point on the earth's surface—say the platform of Grantham station—then the speed of the *Flying Scotsman* as it flashes through the station will have a certain value, perhaps fifty miles per hour. If, however, the man with the stop-watches is observing from another train running in the same direction at precisely the same speed, then, relative to this observer, the speed of the *Flying Scotsman* will be exactly zero. Suppose now that the observer could station himself at some point outside the earth, for example on the sun, then to him the train would share in the velocity of the earth and its speed would be astronomical. The speed of the train is relative to where the observer stations himself. Has it a 'true' speed, or only a speed which depends upon where the observer happens to be? No wonder the puzzled traveller, reading Einstein, said to the railway official, 'Guard, does Rugby stop at this train today?'

We, from our observatory upon the earth, which is in motion in its own orbit and at its own velocity, observe and measure the movements of other bodies, and thus we build up a co-ordinated system of knowledge concerning the mechanics which appear to us to govern the universe. Astronomers and mathematicians have devoted themselves to this task for centuries, but underlying all their results was the assumption that the earth was the only thinkable location for an observatory, and that measurements taken from this vantage point were the only possible set of figures on which to base our knowledge of the universe. Imagine now an observer studying the same phenomena as an earthbound astronomer, but whose telescope is mounted on another star. He is moving at a quite different speed and most, though not all, his observations and calculations will be different. Which set of figures will be correct? Which system of knowledge is the 'true' system? We have not the right to say that it must be *our* system and *our* figures. They are only true according to our frame of reference. The results obtained by a Martian observer (if such exists) are true according to his frame of reference. We may never know which is true 'according to nature'. Indeed most scientists would dismiss the question as meaningless.

The conclusion to be drawn from these experiences is that the scientist is, at one and the same time, an observer and an integral part of what he observes. When as a physician he studies human anatomy or human psychology he is encountering himself. When, as a geologist, paleontologist or biologist, he unravels the intricacies of the evolutionary process, he is examining his own ancestry and telling his own life story. When, as an astronomer, he measures the velocities and pin points the positions of the stars in their courses, he is himself in motion, himself in orbit. He is both the archer handling the bow and the arrow which is shot. This is the rock of what man himself is; a creature free and yet bound.

THE HISTORIAN AS PARTICIPANT

Our double status can also be illustrated from the historian's experience. His interest lies in the development of men and women as persons, and in the communities and institutions which they create, and in the way in which they come to terms with, and make use of, their environment and circumstances. He studies their political and social development, the clash of policies and ambitions, the struggle to establish order, to maintain stability, and to extend the reach of their power. When the historian records all this he is writing about his own past, and he is writing from the standpoint of his own place, and the place of his generation, in an unfolding pattern of events.

The concepts of continuity, and of perpetual change within the continuity, are essential to the historian. The city of London, for example, is a vastly different place in 1965 from the city which the Romans knew. The political realities of post-war Italy are almost wholly other than the struggle between the city states at the time of the Renaissance. Yet there is continuity in the histories of London and of Italy, as well as violent upheaval and peaceful change. The historian, however, lives at a particular time and occupies a particular place in this continuing story, and the time and the place determine what he sees. There is a relativity conditioning the observations of the historian similar to that which conditions the observations of the astronomer. That is why, for example, the history of the later Stuart kings appears so different in the works of Clarendon and Burnet, written in the seventeenth and eighteenth centuries, in the nineteenth century interpretation of Ranke, and in G. N. Clark's twentieth century volume in the *Oxford History of England*. The general array of facts does not greatly differ, but each historian looks at the fortunes of kings and people in this period from the standpoint of his own age, and sees only what his eyes permit him to see. After reading their books we know a great deal about the later Stuarts : it is hardly an exaggeration to say that we know as much about Clarendon, Burnet, Ranke and Clark.

A contemporary historian, E. H. Carr, elaborated this point in the Trevelyan Lectures delivered in the university of Cambridge in 1961. He asked how far historians are single individuals, and how far they are products of their society and their period. His answer was emphatic :

> We sometimes speak of the course of history as 'a moving procession'. The metaphor is fair enough, provided it does not tempt the historian to think of himself as an eagle surveying the scene from a lonely crag or as a V.I.P. at the saluting base. Nothing of the kind! The historian is just another dim figure trudging along in another part of the procession. And as the procession winds along, swinging now to the right and now to the left, and sometimes doubling back on itself, the relative position of different parts of the procession are constantly changing, so that it may make perfectly good sense to say, for example, that we are nearer today to the Middle Ages than were our great grandfathers a century ago, or that the age of Caesar is nearer to us than the age of Dante. New vistas, new angles of vision, constantly appear as the procession —and the historians with it—moves along. The historian is part of history. The point in the procession at which he finds himself determines his angle of vision over the past.[1]

This why R. G. Collingwood argued that 'every generation must re-write history in its own way', and that historians must not only find new answers to old questions, but also revise the questions themselves. He then continued :

> This is not an argument for historical scepticism. It is only the discovery . . . that the historian himself, together with the here and now which forms the total body of evidence available to him, is a part of the process he is studying, has his own place in that process, and can see it only from the point of view which at the present moment he occupies within it.[2]

Man belongs to the past and is moulded by the past. He has his own place in the continuation of the past which is

---

[1] *What is History?* (Pelican ed., 1964), pp. 35-6.
[2] *The Idea of History* (1946), p. 248.

the present. We may, for instance, visit the Roman wall in Northumbria. Standing on those windy uplands we are spectators, detached observers. Yet our lives and our ideas are profoundly influenced by the legacy of Rome of which the wall is a symbol. Roman concepts of justice and of political stability are built into our present-day outlook. As we examine the wall we are like critics in the theatre, seated in the stalls, watching the action of the play with approval or disapproval. But we have also to mount the stage and take an active part in the play of which the Roman defence of Britain was an early scene. In the words of Strindberg :

> Could I but sit among the audience and watch the play!
> But I must mount the stage, take part and act.

Constant change within continuity; a fast flowing river into which no man can step twice—that is the rock of what history is. Historians, and indeed all men of action, have a double status. They are both critics in the stalls and actors upon the stage until they speak their exit line.

THE RELIGIOUS MAN AS PARTICIPANT

Man in his religious life, no less than the scientist and the historian in theirs, is made aware in a variety of ways of his double status.

In the first place, if faith does not forestall experience but arises out of it, then, like the astronomer making observations from his own point in space, and like the historian writing from his own point in time, the religious man searches for God, for his portrait of Jesus, for the meaning of life, as he stands at one point in human history, and lives through one phase of human development. We are challenged to be true to our *present* experience, interpreting it as perceptively as we can. We cannot evade this challenge by taking refuge in 'the faith once delivered to the saints'. The doctrine of revelation does not mean that we have been given a 'deposit of truth' which serves as an infallible authority; a sort of package deal which includes everything, even the meaning of our twentieth-century experience.

It is possible, and highly desirable, for Christians to enter imaginatively into the experience recorded in the Bible and in Christian history, but to understand, by an effort of creative imagination, what Simon Peter thought and felt, does not mean that we can make his experience, in all its fullness, our own. We do not stand at the same point in history as Peter, and we cannot borrow another man's experience of Christ in this fashion. He cannot be for us the metaphysical Christ of the fourth century who was *homoousion* and not *homoiousion*. He does not come to us as the divinized Byzantine emperor whom the makers of the Ravenna mosaics depicted, nor as the tortured victim of the cross whom Grunewald painted in his famous altar piece. He does not come to us, as to the Protestant Reformers, supremely as the Saviour from personal sin, nor as to the ardent reformers of the 1920s, as the perfect Socialist. From the place where I now see him, in my contemporary situation and in the context of this book, Christ is light in a dark place, the deliverer from total doubt. He is the embodiment —the incarnation—of that power, wisdom and compassion which is, I believe, at the roots of things, and the centre of that movement towards unity and reconciliation which is the pattern of life and of history. But I should deny my own argument were I not to recognize the relativity of this interpreted experience.

The truth we discover is relative to our position in space and time. That is one parallel between the experiences given to us in science, history and religion. There is another. As the scientist and the historian are both independent observers and part of the process they observe, so all men have this double relationship whenever they exercise their power of self-consciousness. Alone among created things, man is reflective, aware not only of his surroundings but also of himself. He has the power to stand outside himself and look at his own life. He is, therefore, both the observer and what he observes, and in his moral judgments he is, at one and the same time, both the prosecutor and the defendant. Our double status is clearly revealed whenever we say, 'I was right', or 'I was wrong'.

This has been well argued by Professor John Macmurray.

> This simple fact that we are able and indeed compelled to pass judgment upon ourselves lies very near the centre of the religious field. As pronouncing judgment we are outside the field of experience, but as judged we are inside it. In other words we are both transcendent of experience and immanent in it. This union of transcendence and immanence is, then, the full fact about human personality. It is an empirical fact and a natural fact.[1]

There is a third parallel between our experiences in science, history and religion. Not only are we transcendent as observers and immanent as part of what we observe; as religious men we are free and yet bound.

The most vivid religious statement of this experience is to be found in two myths in the early chapters of the Book of Genesis: the myth of creation and the myth of man's fall. In the first of these it is said that man is made in God's image, and it is also said that he has been given dominion over all created things. The statement that man is made in God's image is capable of many interpretations, but since it occurs in the context of God's creative activity in forming the universe, it certainly means that man, like God, is a creator. As there is no greater thing that can be said about God than that he makes things, so no greater thing can be

[1] *The Structure of Religious Experience*, p. 38.

said about man. And man is not only a creator; he is responsible and he is free. He has been given control on earth; he has dominion 'over every living thing that moveth upon the earth'. This sign of God's graciousness was always a source of wonder to the Hebrews, and their gratitude at being given freedom and responsibility is revealed in many places in the Bible.

It is, however, God who creates man in his own image, bestowing upon him freedom and responsibility. Moreover, there is a limitation imposed upon his power of control. There is one tree in paradise the fruit of which he may not eat. Man is not only a creator but also a creature. He has dominion over the earth but is himself under the dominion of God. This is his double status expressed in religious language. We recognize the first by accepting responsibility and participating in the world of action. We recognize the second by worship and obedience.

There are contemporary theologians who reject, as secular Humanists reject, this double status of freedom and dependence. Using a phrase of Dietrich Bonhoeffer's they say that man has now 'come of age' and no longer feels dependent upon God. God has shown his graciousness by withdrawing from the scene of human action and by bestowing upon us unlimited freedom. This is without doubt the prevailing feeling of our time, but Bonhoeffer's phrase is a curious one. The desire to be autonomous is a mark of adolescence, not of maturity. It is the teenager with urgent desires but limited experience who claims absolute freedom. Mature men more frequently recognize the peril of possessing unlimited freedom and unchecked power. The myth of the fall, in which man loses paradise because he seizes the power which does not belong to him, and eats the forbidden fruit in order that he may be as a god, does not stand alone. Many of the great myths of literature, Daedalus and Icarus, the

Faust myth, J. R. R. Tolkien's *The Lord of the Rings*, reflect man's deep experience of his double status, and point to the peril which threatens those who rebel against it by seizing unlimited power. But perhaps in a world split in two and armed with atomic weapons, we do not need the insights of the great myths to convince us of the inevitable disasters which beset a civilization in which rival men and conflicting interests are driven into headlong conflicts by a desire for power which recognizes no limits.

There is at the root of things a rock of what man himself is, and it shapes his freedom with a necessary answer. He is both the archer handling the bow and the arrow which is shot; both the critic in the stalls and the actor upon the stage; both the prosecutor and the defendant; both creator and creature.

When Michelangelo painted the creation of man on the ceiling of the Sistine Chapel he expressed perfectly this experience of being, at one and the same time, both creator and created. With infinite tenderness God reaches out a finger towards the first man, and with love and wonder Adam stretches out his finger towards his creator. Man and God respond perfectly to each other, but their fingers do not quite touch. Man remains free but across that tiny gap, between the finger of the creator and the finger of the created, power and love, like an electric spark, can leap from the one to the other.

6

THE INNER AND THE OUTER
SHAPE

I T I S the argument of this chapter that there is an illuminating parallel to be drawn between the concept of evolution and the history of the Jewish people as it is told in the Bible. This will sound like the oddest of all odd associations; the maddest of juxtapositions between two series of events which not only appear to have nothing in common but which, in the past, have been held to contradict one another. Was there not in the nineteenth century a famous controversy which in the popular mind was summed up in the slogan, 'Darwin versus the Bible'?

The point of connection between evolution and the biblical story is that they are examples of the truth that both in nature and in history there is a depth of meaning which can only be fully grasped when we recognize that there are surface events which can be observed by the ordinary techniques of the scientist and the historian, and also submerged connections which are only revealed when they rise to the surface. It is in this inter-play between the outer and the inner shape of nature and of history that we discern their full significance.

THE 'WITHIN' OF EVOLUTION

The concept of evolution, in its widest sense, is one of the most magnificent achievements of the human mind and imagination. It fits together into one vast conceptual scheme innumerable detailed observations from many branches of science, and because it illuminates the past it gives significance to our present experience and points towards the future of mankind. It is more than a theory about the way in which living organisms have developed from earlier to more recent forms. It is the pattern of the universe. The most ancient star and tomorrow's child are linked together in one unfolding process. It is not an immutable pattern laid down from the beginning of time, but one which is changing, developing and becoming more complex.

Whether the universe had a beginning in time, perhaps twelve thousand million years ago, or whether there has been a continuous creation of matter does not affect the present argument. It is enough for our purpose to recall the galaxies, about a hundred million of them; to recall also the solar system with the planets in their orbits round the sun; the emergence on the earth of living creatures, and the arrival of *Homo sapiens*, a creature formed by natural selection working over vast spans of time. All these are stages in one continuing process.

It is easy to miss, or even to repudiate, the immense significance of the pattern. The diversities and ramifications are so innumerable that a scientist working in the specialized fields of biology, zoology, geology or paleontology must concern himself with such questions as the mutations of genes and the structure of the chromosomes. He must concentrate upon such small details of the pattern as the transforming of a reptile's leg into a bird's wing, or the change in the structure of an ape's pelvis which enabled the improved species to walk upright on its hind legs, and to hold tools and weapons in its free hands. Such technical matters and detailed studies provide the evidence that there is a pattern but by their complexity they may also prevent us from seeing it.

When we look at this vast and intricate process from the standpoint of our own place within it as men and women, we can see that so far there have been three critical points. The first of these was the formation of the earth, destined to become our home. The second was the emergence of living creatures. The third, which is the most significant for this argument, was the emergence of the creature *Homo sapiens*, distinguished from all others by the power of thought. When we examine the oldest human artifacts, the flint weapons and tools sharpened to a point or ground to an edge, or gaze upon the virile springing animals which early man painted upon the walls of his caves, we are observing the evidence for the birth of thought. There was a moment when creatures reflected, and on reflection realized that a sharp weapon is better than a blunt one, and that possibly there exist mysterious powers which can be enlisted to ensure successful hunting. This birth of thought was a critical point in evolution, and when man passed it he was separated from all other creatures. Many of his activities were (and still are) those of other animals. He struggles for survival, for food, for power. He knows sexual excitement and satisfaction. He lives in groups, accepting their customs and prohibitions, but when he passed the critical point all these activities were marvellously enriched because now he could reflect upon them, and by reflection extend and deepen them.

'The birth of thought' is a vague phrase. Let us give to it a more precise meaning. Man, as distinct from the higher primates, has the capacity for self-awareness. He is not only aware of his environment as animals are, he is aware of himself. He not only knows; he knows that he knows. Again he has the power of conceptual thought and the language in which to express it. Other animals can communicate with each other, but no animal except man has to a high degree the power of abstract reasoning, of recognizing the relationship between different abstract ideas, of constructing theories and testing their validity.

When the critical point was passed another world was born—the world of science and technology, of historical understanding, of the arts, philosophy and religion. Inhabiting this world of the mind are persons, living in their own private kingdoms, yet able to enter into communion with others.

All this is the outer shape of the evolutionary process, but there is in this description a difficulty which is often unrecognized or evaded. It is part of the scientific theory that nothing is created in the evolutionary process, but rather that what is already present is modified, adapted, transmuted into something else. The question therefore arises: What then has been modified to form in man what we call mind? Moreover, and this is an important extension of the same point, our knowledge suggests that the universe is all of a piece. The most distant star, the most ancient rock, the new-born lamb, and the latest child of the human race are all compounded of the same fundamental stuff. All of them are physics and chemistry. The common basic elements—the atoms and molecules—are differently arranged in a nebula and a human being, but this cannot mean that man is an unusual sort of star. The early echinoderms are the ancestors of the mammals, including man, but a human being is not a sort of sea-urchin.

One way of solving this riddle is to play down the unique fact of human self-awareness. It is sometimes said that science has no room for values, and therefore there is no justification for saying that a man is of greater significance than a water flea. This is one of the occasional scientific statements which are simply untrue to human experience.

Another solution is to play down the unique fact of human self-consciousness by concentrating exclusively upon man's physical features. It is fashionable today to write an article on the structure of the mind and to discuss nothing but the physiology of the brain and the central nervous system. It is of course undeniable that what we call mind has a physical basis, but the attempt, sustained over recent years, to explain man's unique reflective powers in purely physical terms, remains wholly unconvincing.

> The mental is not examinable as a form of energy. That in brief is the gap which parts psychiatry and physiology. No mere running round the cycle of 'forms of energy' takes us across that chasm.[1]

This statement was made in the Gifford Lectures for 1937-8, and in the intervening years a great deal more work has been done on the brain and the central nervous system, but Sir Charles Sherrington's dictum has not been disproved.

An alternative way of solving the riddle is to postulate the existence of mind, in rudimentary form, in the earlier stages of evolution. This safeguards the principle that the universe is all of a piece and recognizes the unique quality of human self-consciousness. If the evidence for this solution is meagre, that may well be because scientists by inclination and training look mainly upon the outer shape of things. But if it is meagre it is not wholly absent. Sherrington, for example, quotes the Spanish neurologist, Cajal, who gave special study to the retina and nerve lines to the brain in the eyes of insects, hoping that there he might discover, in a relatively simple form, a knowledge of the way animals see. After two years' study he wrote of the immense complexity of the structure of the insects' eyes, and he concluded :

> Peering through the microscope into this Lilliputian life one wonders whether what we disdainfully term 'instinct' (Berg-

[1] *Man on his Nature* (1951 ed.), p. 228.

son's 'intuition') is not, as Jules Fabre claims, life's crowning mental gift. Mind with instant and decisive action, the mind which in these tiny and ancient beings reached its blossom ages ago and earliest of all.[1]

Again, in 1932, J. B. S. Haldane wrote in an essay on *Science and Ethics* :

> We do not find obvious evidence of life or mind in so-called inert matter, and we naturally study them most easily where they are most completely manifested; but if the scientific point of view is correct we shall ultimately find them, at least in rudimentary form, all through the universe.[2]

One of the most recent expositions of this view is in *The Phenomenon of Man*, by Pierre Teilhard de Chardin, the French paleontologist and Jesuit priest. He tells us that he had already been working along this line when he read the passage from J. B. S. Haldane. From his study emerged the vision that every phenomenon has a 'within aspect' as well as a 'without', though, he argued, up to now science has never troubled to look at the world except from without.

The point in the evolutionary process where the 'within' and the 'without' of phenomena is unmistakable is, of course, the point where man emerges. Looked at from 'without' he is an organism endowed with physical energy and compounded of the same common chemicals as all things organic and inorganic alike. Looked at from 'without' he has a highly developed brain and nervous system. But looked at from 'within' he is mind, consciousness, psychic and spiritual energy. Working backwards from this analysis Teilhard de Chardin argued that there is a lining to all things like the lining of a well-made coat.

> It is impossible to deny that, deep within ourselves, an 'interior' appears at the heart of things, as it were seen through

[1] *Op. cit.*, pp. 108-9.
[2] Quoted by de Chardin, p. 57.

a rent. This is enough to ensure that, in one degree or another, this 'interior' should obtrude itself as existing everywhere in nature from all time. Since the stuff of the universe has an inner aspect at one point of itself, there is necessarily *a double aspect to its structure*, that is to say in every region of space and time . . . *co-extensive with their Without, there is a Within to things*.[1]

It is a serious defect of de Chardin's book that he did not think it necessary to give examples of those moments in the evolutionary process when, as in Cajal's work on insects, the 'within' rises to the surface. His argument, however, should not be rejected out of hand for this reason. What is needed is more evidence from those trained to search for it. De Chardin is saying that as we go backwards in time from man through the successive stages of evolution, back to the first organisms, back to the earth fiery hot, back to the stars and galaxies there will be a within of things, though attenuated to the uttermost. This does not mean that atoms and molecules have vestigial minds. De Chardin was fond of using the analogy from physics of a change of state. When a liquid is heated there comes a critical point at which it changes its state; it boils and turns into a gas : water turns into steam. Yet there is a fundamental continuity between the liquid and the gas. In atoms and molecules the 'within' is negligible, and the scientific description of them is all that we can possess. At a certain level of organization, in the living cell, there occurs a change of state. New properties emerge. At a higher level still consciousness is born.

The inner shape of a continuing process is not to be thought of in the same way as, for example, a fairy godmother is concealed within the rags of an old witch. The outer shape is not a mere appearance of the inner reality. Both possess reality, and without an understanding of both

[1] *The Phenomenon of Man* (1959), p. 56. Author's italics.

the nature of the universe is only partially revealed. At a certain stage, however, as will be argued in the final chapter, when mind and self-consciousness are well developed, the 'within' becomes the directing force of the process. At this point one may speak not of one process, but of one action.

The universe is all of a piece. Teilhard de Chardin had his own solution concerning the relationship between the 'within' and the 'without' of things, which he admitted was tentative, and which is probably unacceptable. But

> in the world nothing could ever burst forth as final across the different thresholds successively traversed by evolution (however critical they be), which has not already existed in an obscure and primordial way.[1]

The universe is one. That conviction inspired de Chardin as it does all scientists, but can the vision be substantiated unless nature has both an inner and an outer shape?

THE INNER SHAPE OF BIBLICAL HISTORY

The events recorded in the Old and New Testaments, like the events of any other historical period, were the outcome of human actions within a particular environment. The sense of man's responsibility for the conduct of the world over which he has been given dominion, is central in biblical thought. Yet the biblical writers also claim to have uncovered the directing forces of history, and to see in the story of the people of Israel and of the Christian Church, a shape, a rhythm, a divine purpose. For them history has a meaning; a pattern can be discerned within it. The modern reader of the Bible may reject this pattern. He may be unable to see meaning or to believe in the divine purpose, but to ignore the claim is to misunderstand the documents.

There is nothing in the outer shape of the biblical story

[1] *The Phenomenon of Man*, p. 71.

which is unfamiliar to the historian. At the beginning of the Early Iron Age, round about 1200 BC, a loose confederation of nomadic tribes, Semite by race, infiltrated by slow degrees into the land of Canaan. In comparison with the Canaanites with their walled cities, their armoured chariots, their knowledge of an alphabetic form of writing and their trade with Egypt and Mesopotamia, these nomadic tribesmen were uncivilized barbarians, landless men, who lived in tents and whose wealth was in sheep and goats. Yet they had a certain core of strength, derived from traditions of their past, which enabled them to respond to the challenge of the situation with a tenacious and obstinate power, and finally to overcome their more sophisticated neighbours. These traditions told the story of the patriarchs who, centuries before, had lived a nomadic life in this land : they also told of a great deliverance, nearer in time, when some of the tribesmen who had been slaves in Egypt, had been enabled to escape from Pharaoh's bondage.

Under the leadership of a remarkable king named David this loose confederation of tribes was welded into a nation with its capital in Jerusalem. It enjoyed a brief spell of prosperity and international prestige, and then followed a long succession of disasters. There were internal strains which led to the division of the kingdom into two unequal parts, Israel in the north with its capital at Samaria, and Judah in the south with David's city of Jerusalem as its centre. Another short period of prosperity followed before first Israel and then Judah were sucked into the whirlpools of international politics, caught helplessly in the rushing waters of Assyrian, Babylonian and Egyptian expansion, and both were destroyed. Israel vanished from the political map : Judah, with most of its people in exile in Babylon, clung on to its national identity, and was restored by the clemency of Cyrus, king of Persia, a pale shadow of its former self, to exist precariously as the plaything of contending empires, until finally it fell under the dominion of Rome.

At this point the sequence of national events—the rise to power, the years of decline, the subjugation by new emerging peoples—is sharply interrupted by the story of an obscure Galilean carpenter, said to be of the royal line of David, a prophet and healer, who steadfastly refused to take part in revolutionary politics, but who was crucified by the Roman governor as a suspected rebel. His few followers, who on the arrest of Jesus had gone into hiding, reappeared in Jerusalem some six weeks later proclaiming that their master had risen from the dead and was invisibly present with them. Out of this new faith in a crucified, risen and ever-present Lord came the Christian Church, and the first few years of its unfinished story are reflected in the second half of the New Testament.

There is nothing in this sequence of events to surprise the historian. The coalescence of related tribes into a nation; the rise to power of that new community; its failure to hold its own in the struggle with more vigorous peoples; the emergence of a new faith which injects remarkable power into those who embrace it—all this is the standard stuff of history. What must challenge the historian is the bold interpretation put upon these events by the authors of his documents. They declare that these things happened, not merely through the interplay of political, social and personal forces, but because God, by means of these historical forces, was through the centuries shaping and perfecting his 'definite plan' for mankind.

This bold interpretation is, of course, vulnerable and easily challenged. The outer shape of Israel's history is, for the most part, just like the story of other ambitious but unsuccessful nations in its bid for power. The biblical writers, like those who inscribed the records of other ancient peoples, often claim the sanction of their God for acts of violent aggression and downright cruelty. If we are to find permanent meaning in these documents we must give up the notion that God takes sides in battles and political manoeuvres, and gives success to the nation he favours. What possible justification can there be, then, for claiming that in these events, to a degree not found in other sequences of events, there is revealed the will and purpose of Being-Itself as Gracious? The claim can only be defended if we look below the surface to the inner shape of this stretch of history. As there is a hidden chain reaction in the evolutionary process which breaks surface most clearly and dramatically in human consciousness, so hidden deep below the surface events of biblical history there is a chain reaction initiated by the activity of God. At intervals it comes to the surface and an outward event glows with new light and is charged with eternal meaning. In this inner shape the pattern of history is disclosed and the revelation is given.

The pattern revealed by the inner shape of biblical events can be summed up in the two words, 'unity' and 'reconciliation'. These are not exclusively religious words. They describe the essentials of any pattern whether in nature, in art, or in a man's personal relationships, and they are the great structural lines of the inner shape of biblical history. The 'definite plan' of God, the Lord of history, is here revealed as the bringing together of disparate parts and contending elements in a cluster of relationships, and it is the divine will that these relationships shall govern the life of man with man, and of man with God. At the beginning of the biblical record this revelation is given in matter of fact terms and in down to earth incidents. It increases in depth and complexity as the centuries pass and reaches a profundity of meaning as St Paul reflects upon it. 'He (Christ) is before all things and in him all things hold together' (Col. 1.17).

The pattern of unity and reconciliation extends over some eighteen centuries from Abraham, that wandering nomad whom later generations of Israelites acknowledged as the father of their nation, to Christ and on into the early years of the Christian Church. For long periods of time it is underground, but it emerges sufficiently often for us to be able to identify it, and to observe its growing power and complexity.

The inner shape of biblical history begins with the birth of a new nation, formed out of Abraham's nomadic tribe, upon which is laid the task of being the mediator of God's blessing 'to all the families of the earth'. This, it has been said, is like a command to history. There is no limit to the extent of the divine blessing; it embraces the whole international community, at all times, in all places. But to resist the pattern of unity and reconciliation is to bring a curse upon oneself (Gen. 12.1-3). Abraham, according to the story, accepted the task. In Mesopotamia, from whence he had migrated, each aggressive city state tried constantly to enrich itself at the expense of its neighbours. In Palestine conflicts amongst the nomads over grazing rights and the possession of wells were common enough. Abraham, however, was a man of peace. His words to his graceless nephew Lot might well be his motto, 'Let there be no strife.' In the warlike and aggressive setting of the time his justice and generosity seem a strange anachronism. In his everyday dealings with his neighbours he set himself to live within the purpose of unity and reconciliation, and to become a mediator of the blessing.

Abraham may well be an historical character, but the record of his life in the Book of Genesis is not well-documented history. It is an ancient saga. It is this which gives the Abraham story its value because a saga reveals the inward intuitive interpretation which a community puts upon the deepest realities of its life. It reflects a people's historical experience much more vividly than do the official records of wars, migrations and political disasters. To quote a writer on Homer, a saga comprises 'the sum total of the living historical recollection of peoples. In it is mirrored, in fact and in truth, the history of a people. It is the form in which a people thinks of its own history.'[1]

The saga of Abraham reveals to us the deepest religious experience of a nation in its infancy. This is what the first Israelites knew about God and his purpose. He is a gracious God towards all men, and they are the mediators of his blessing. For many centuries this historical experience was preserved largely in the memories of the tribesmen. For long periods, no doubt, it was deep underground. It rose again to the surface about 800 BC when a highly creative writer whom scholars call the Yahwist, because he consistently used the name Yahweh for God, saw deeply into its meaning and gave it imperishable literary form.

It is usually held that the history of Israel, as distinct from saga narratives, begins with the life and work of Moses. The two most important events in his leadership were the exodus from Egypt and the Covenant, made at Sinai, between God and the tribesmen. Certainly these constituted a highly significant development in the outer shape of Israel's history, but in these events there is no disclosure of the inner shape; no hint of the universal blessing of which Israel was the mediator. In circumstances of slavery, and later of persistent hostility from other nomadic tribes, conquest through war becomes the Israelites' objective. The covenant with Abraham is ignored. The 'God of Abraham' now appears as the warlike protector of a 'chosen people', and the conception

---

[1] Quoted from Finsler's *Homer* in G. von Rad, *Genesis* (Eng. ed., 1961), p. 31. The exposition by von Rad of the role of the saga repays study.

of 'the people of God' changes its character. The fatal delusion which was so often to distort Israel's religion now arises. To be 'the holy nation', bound by the Covenant on Sinai, meant that in return for moral and cultic obedience God would give victory in war and prosperity in the promised land. During these years the pattern of unity and reconciliation ran underground.

It was the great prophets who reinterpreted the phrase 'a holy nation' in the light of the covenant of Abraham. Amos, the earliest of them, was mainly concerned with national unity and with social justice, prerequisite reforms if Israel was to become again the mediator of the blessing. The pattern of universal unity reappears in the prophecies of Isaiah, counsellor to successive kings of Judah in the eighth century BC, and in the words of a prophet whose name we do not know who lived in exile in Babylon, and whose utterances are preserved in chapters xl-lv of the Book of Isaiah.

The situation in the Middle East in the eighth to the sixth centuries BC was far more confused and explosive than in the nomadic days of Abraham. It was a world of great contending empires, expanding wealth and commerce, with ever-increasing opportunities for nations and individuals to seek power and possessions. In this situation the interpretation of the divine purpose handed down in the Abraham saga was correspondingly complex and profound.

Throughout the years of political crisis and great danger from aggressive Assyrian kings and untrustworthy Egyptian Pharaohs, Isaiah used his influence at the royal court of Judah to press upon successive kings a policy of neutrality. Judah should pay tribute to Assyria when it was unavoidable, turn a deaf ear to the blandishments of Egypt, and refuse to enter into alliances with other small states. This advice to withdraw from the political scramble (it was repeated in later years by the prophet Jeremiah) was always highly unpopular, an offence to the pride and prestige of kings and counsellors. It was in fact the only realistic policy, but Isaiah was not merely being politically prudent. His major concern as a prophet of God was that Judah should be an instrument of the divine purpose of unity and recon- ciliation, and the values which motivated aggressive nations were incompatible with the distinctive part which his nation had to play in God's 'definite plan'. Judah was to be a 'holy nation', reconciled to God and united within itself by social justice. It was to be an instrument of peace in a war-ridden world. In a famous poem, which also appears in the Book of Micah, Isaiah painted a picture of all the nations flowing into Jerusalem, ascending the hill of the Lord, and sharing in God's purpose by beating swords into ploughshares and spears into pruning hooks (Isa. 2.2-5). In an even more striking prophecy he re-echoed the promise of the saga of Abraham : 'In thee shall all the families of the earth be blessed.'

> In that day there will be a highway from Egypt to Assyria, and the Assyrian will come into Egypt, and the Egyptian into Assyria, and the Egyptians will worship with the Assyrians. In that day Israel will be the third with Egypt and Assyria, a blessing in the midst of the earth, whom the Lord of hosts has blessed, saying, 'Blessed be Egypt my people, and Assyria the work of my hands, and Israel my heritage' (*Isa.* 19.23-4).

Isaiah was a visionary, but he was also a realist. He knew what happens to small nations like Judah when great em- pires are on the march. He knew that without extreme political wisdom they will be forced to fight; may even win a battle or two, and survive a crisis, but in the end they will suffer defeat. He knew also that powerful kingdoms like Assyria over-reach themselves and crash into ruins. But he believed that a small nation can have its own particular part

D

to play in world affairs, and that it was the task of Judah to be an instrument of reconciliation. And he held fast to his belief, projecting it into the future.

> Therefore thus says the Lord, who redeemed Abraham, concerning the house of Jacob:
>   'Jacob shall no more be ashamed,
>   no more shall his face grow pale.
>   For when he sees his children,
>   the work of my hands, in his midst,
>   they will sanctify my name;
>   they will sanctify the Holy One of Jacob,
>   and will stand in awe of the God of Israel.
>   And those who err in spirit will come to understanding,
>   and those who murmur will accept instruction' (*Isa.* 29. 22-24).

About one hundred and forty years after Isaiah's death, in the darkest days of the exile in Babylon, a prophet who is generally called the Second Isaiah saw even deeper into the inner history of his nation. If Judah was to fulfil its destiny as a mediator of the blessing to others, it could only do so through the acceptance of suffering. A people who will 'bring forth justice to the nations' must accept defeat in battle and injustice in captivity in such a manner that its sufferings become transmuted into redemptive power. In the famous Servant Songs which appear in the second part of the Book of Isaiah, such suffering, undeserved yet freely accepted, will 'startle many nations'. If the purpose is to be fulfilled the Servant nation must be wounded for the transgressions of other peoples, and bruised for their iniquities, that by its stripes they may be healed (*Isa.* 52.13-53.12). Only then will 'the chosen nation' be 'a light to the nations, that God's salvation may reach to the ends of the earth' (*Isa.* 46.6).

The history of the years which followed the exile in Babylon is complicated and confused. It is clear, however, that the remnant of the Jews who returned to Palestine and attempted to rebuild their national life on very meagre resources, were in no mood to recall the experience of their ancestors who had treasured the Abraham saga. Yet in this time of uncompromising and exclusive nationalism one man at least remembered the true function of his people. He was the author of the Book of Jonah, a parable about a Jew bidden to travel to his nation's enemies and oppressors and to offer them the unity which comes when men worship together the same God. But in the grim years of the Seleucid rule in Palestine, throughout the horror of the Maccabean revolt, and on to the subjugation of the nation by the Romans, the Jews, naturally enough, turned inward upon themselves. The outer shape of their history in these four centuries is a desperate struggle to preserve some at least of the features of their national life. The inner shape, which alone gives their history permanent significance, went underground until it broke surface again, now in the fullness of its power, in the life and teaching of a Jew born when Quirinius was Governor of Syria, and executed when Pontius Pilate was Procurator of Judaea.

The Roman names of these officials symbolize the political realities of the time of Jesus. Under the dominion of Rome the Jewish nation in these years was torn by factions and stretched by tensions almost to breaking point. In Jerusalem the Sadducean party, composed for the most part of wealthy and aristocratic families, played a subtle game of diplomacy designed to secure for themselves what Rome had left of Israel's authority and power. Throughout the country the Pharisees strove, in the face of the Roman occupation, to preserve the national identity and the traditional religion. In Galilee, especially, there was a strong undercurrent of militant nationalism with revolutionary outbreaks, bands of armed men, and sporadic acts of violence. Some of the grievances of these groups were economic, but for the most part it was the old political itch for independence and power which stirred them. The kingdom would be restored to Israel; the glories of king David and the magnificence of king Solomon would shine again in Jesusalem when the Romans were driven into the sea.

Jesus faced these political realities as the Yahwist writer, as Isaiah, as the unnamed prophet, and as the author of the Book of Jonah had done by going back to the original experience of his race in the saga of Abraham, but he recreated the experience in a unique way for himself and for his followers. Brought up in the revolutionary atmosphere of Galilee, and conscious of possessing remarkable powers of leadership, he decisively rejected, both for himself and for his nation, the aspirations of political power. In this, as in so much else, he adopted the standpoint of the Old Testament prophets. He too was a realist who saw that for Israel to join the struggle for power meant annihilation. He too was a dedicated Servant of the Lord who recognized that men's ambitions are destructive of the ways of God. With the rejection came a positive challenge to the nation, for he declared that it was now face to face with the supreme crisis of its history. It was confronted, he said, by nothing less than the kingdom of God, here and now in its midst, and it must decide whether to accept or to refuse it. 'The time has come, the kingdom of God is upon you. Repent and believe the Good News.'

In his teaching about the kingdom the thought of Jesus moved on more than one level. Our immediate concern is with the kingly rule, the sovereignty of God, as a present experience which challenged the peasants and fishermen of Galilee, the merchants of the cities, the Pharisees, the politicians and the would-be revolutionaries. It was a challenge presented by Christ's own presence as a prophet and healer; his coming and his deeds had inaugurated the kingdom. 'If I, by the finger of God, drive out the demons, then be sure that the kingdom of God has already come upon you' (*Luke* 11.20).

Israel, therefore, was confronted by the supreme crisis of its history; a crisis provoked by the coming of Jesus. Now the inner shape of the nation's history, glimpsed from afar by patriarchs and prophets, was fully exposed to view. The underground chain reaction had emerged into the light of day.

> Truly I say unto you, many prophets and righteous men have longed to see what you see, and did not see it, and to hear what you hear, and did not hear it (*Matt.* 13.17).

The seed which is the kingdom had been growing in secret, but now the harvest had come (*Mark* 4.26-29).

What was the choice confronting Israel? Jesus spoke of the broad way which leads to destruction. No doubt he was thinking of many things—the private follies, ambitions and sins of individuals—but would it be wrong to suppose that he also had in his mind the different forms of nationalism which prevented his people from accepting the kingdom? He spoke also of the narrow way, his own way, which leads to life. Israel might listen to the clamorous voices of Judas of Gamala, the revolutionary leader, of Caiaphas the High Priest, or of Simon the Pharisee and build its house upon sand, or it might take heed to Jesus and build its house upon rock.

The narrow way, the foundation rock, was the divine purpose of unity and reconciliation first disclosed in the saga of Abraham. It was the way trodden by the meek, the sorrowful, the hungry after righteousness, the merciful, the pure in heart, the peacemakers and the persecuted who inherit the kingdom (*Matt.* 5.5-11). It was the way of forgiveness:

If you are offering your gift at the altar and there remember that your brother has something against you, leave your gift there before the altar and go: first be reconciled to your brother and then come and offer your gift (*Matt.* 5.23-24).

In the same spirit of reconciliation Jesus refused to endorse the traditional judgment, fostered by the strictness of the Pharisees, which cast out from society 'tax-collectors' who worked for Herod or for Rome, and 'sinners' who were either immoral or who disregarded the Law and the traditions. He also refused to endorse the national antipathies. He befriended a Roman centurion, declaring that he had a faith not to be found in Israel, and his most provocative parable was about a hated Samaritan who befriended a wounded Jew.

Jesus was always a realist and he knew that his teaching and way of life constituted a challenge to all the deep-rooted attitudes of his nation. He knew that the fierce rays of this opposition would be focused, as in a burning glass, upon his own person, and that he would be consumed. Towards the end of his brief public ministry he seems to have accepted for himself the role of the Suffering Servant. Despised and rejected of men, wounded for their transgressions, bruised for their iniquities, a man of sorrows and acquainted with grief—all this would be fulfilled in his Passion. He went to his death believing in his victory, trusting that through the cross he would become the centre of unity and reconciliation between God and man, and between brothers in one divine family.

Some thirty years later the apostle Paul reflected upon the meaning of Christ's death and expressed his thoughts in language of splendid eloquence. He wrote as a Jew to non-Jews, and he was acutely conscious of the hostility and even contempt with which his own proud nation regarded all other races. This contempt was symbolized for him by a wall in the Temple at Jerusalem which separated the court of the Gentiles from the rest of the building. Jesus had once declared that the Temple was intended to be a 'house of prayer for all nations', but the penalty was death for a non-Jew who passed the gate in the wall. Paul knew from his experience of the first Christian churches that Christ has broken down that 'dividing wall of hostility'. In Ephesus and Corinth, from Antioch in Syria to Rome in Europe, non-Jews who had been 'alienated from the commonwealth of Israel and strangers from the covenant of promise', were now reconciled to Jews by Christ's death. They were no longer 'strangers and foreigners, but fellow-citizens with the saints and members of the household of God' (*Eph.* 2.12-20). When the Lord's Supper was celebrated he saw Jews, Greeks, Syrians, Egyptians, Romans sharing the same bread and drinking from the same cup.

Paul carried his thought much deeper than this rejoicing at an accomplished fact of reconciliation, which was after all only within the fellowship of a minority group in the Empire. This new unity within the Church was a revelation, in a concrete act, of the ultimate truth of things. In it he saw the ordering, the economy, the management of the world's history : the reunion of all things in Christ.

> God has made known to us his hidden purpose—such was his will and pleasure determined beforehand in Christ—to put into effect when the time was ripe : namely that the universe, all in heaven and on earth, might be brought into a unity in Christ (*Eph.* 1.9).

The centre of this unity is Jesus Christ who made peace by the blood of his cross, destroying by a greater power the forces which make for disunion. He stands at the centre of God's economy of the world : he is all in all.

Through him God chose to reconcile the whole universe to himself, making peace by the shedding of his blood upon the cross—to reconcile all things, whether on earth or in heaven, through him alone (*Col.* 1.19-20).

In Christ all things hold together. That is the inner shape of universal history.

7

THE UNIVERSAL PATTERN

'EXPERIENCE', wrote Henry James, 'is never limited, and it is never complete : it is an immense sensibility, a kind of huge spider-web of the finest silken threads suspended in a chamber of consciousness, and catching every air-borne particle in its tissue.'

When we appeal to our experience we are not usually thinking of isolated incidents, but rather of a body of experience in which, over the years, many single encounters have been related in a kind of pattern. Experience grows, but like a tree it grows to a shape. It is to coherent experience that we appeal, in which the different elements are linked together as the threads of a spider's web.

The quest for a web of experience lies behind the activities of scientists, historians and men of religion, for without coherence our experiences are, in the final analysis, meaningless. The search is an arduous one, for in every subject knowledge increases, experience widens, and specialization within narrow fields is inevitable. Nevertheless, the important questions today in science, history and religion are not about details, and not about causes, but about relationships. What, we must ask, is the place of this new thread of knowledge in the web of what is already certainly known? It has been the avowed aim of many scientists to find, or to create, the pattern. 'I now demonstrate', said Newton, 'the frame of the system of the world.' Things were easier at the end of the seventeenth century, but Einstein in the twentieth had the same ambition. 'The object of all science is to co-ordinate our experiences and to bring them into a logical system.'

Historians are more divided about the need or the possibility of tracing out a unified pattern of human activities. H. A. L. Fisher in the often quoted preface to his *History of Europe* denied that there is in history 'a plot, a rhythm, a predetermined pattern', and saw 'only one emergency following upon another'. There is an influential school of contemporary historians which rejects all philosophical notions of pattern as a useless craving for unity and symmetry. Pure research is the aim of these historians, for whom ten years is well spent in examining, let us say, the twelfth-century charters of the abbeys of Lorraine.

In the eyes of other historians this sort of activity is mere fact finding, and facts are useless until they are interpreted. Yet any interpretation, however simple, is an attempt at co-ordination, a linking of events in sequence, and this is the beginning of a pattern. Historians of the second school depict in their books a portrait of an age and write history in the round. Yet however elaborate the pattern worked out in such books, it is obviously incomplete. A man who writes a history of the Middle Ages knows that the points at which he begins and ends his story are both arbitrary dates. The threads of the spider's web which he is examining run back into the ancient world and project forward into the modern age. The history men write is chopped up into segments : 'the Carolingian Period' or the 'Hanoverians', but history as men live it is one vast, complex, moving process in which decisions taken in one century work themselves out in future centuries, and events occurring in a particular place and at a particular time trigger off chain reactions which run underground, as it were, to reappear and influence other events and other men far distant in space and time. There is no escape from the pattern of history, though for lack of knowledge or skill or time we may fail to exhibit it.

If it is true, as I have argued in chapter 4, that religious experience arises out of everyday experience common to all men, and if any encounter which confronts a human being may be a pathway to God, then the religious man is bound to seek for the underlying unity which may bind together all phenomena and every experience. That is why he must seek to understand, and to learn from, the work of scientists and historians, and indeed from every kind of experience. His basic hypothesis, for which he ought to seek evidence with enthusiasm and with rigour, is that all experience is ultimately derived from one source—from the activity of God. The scientific 'frame of the world' and the spider-thread of history both have their roots in the divine activity. In theological language, it is in Christ that 'all things hold together'.

In the article already quoted, J. Robert Oppenheimer defined the basic characteristics of the scientific pattern:

> The unity consists of two things: first and ever more strikingly, an absence of inconsistency. Thus we may talk of life in terms of purpose, adaptation and function, but we have found in living things no tricks played upon the laws of physics and chemistry. We have found, and I expect will find, a total consistency, and between the different subjects, even as remote as genetics and topology, an occasional sharp mutual relevance. They throw light on each other; they have something to do with each other; often the greatest things in the sciences occur when two different discoveries, made in different worlds, turn out to have so much in common that they are examples of a still greater discovery.
>
> The image is not that of an ordered array of facts in which every one somehow follows from a more fundamental one. It is rather that of a living thing; a tree doing something which trees do not normally do, occasionally having the branches grow together and part again in a great network.[1]

[1] *Encounter*, October 1962, pp. 6-7.

In the argument of this chapter I extend this definition to embrace not simply scientific experience but our total human experience. To believe that there is a unity which binds together all phenomena and every encounter, whether it be in science, history or religion, it is not necessary to demonstrate that all the facts can be arranged in an ordered sequence. It is not that kind of a pattern. We should search for evidence of an over-all consistency of experience, though since our knowledge is growing and our experience enlarging at a phenomenal rate, there are at present too many contradictions for us to find 'total consistency'. What we do possess is experience in common, and an occasional sharp mutual relevance.

THE STRUCTURAL LINE OF THE PATTERN

There are many spiders webs disclosed by science. There are, for example, intricate and aesthetically pleasing patterns in mathematics. In biology there are subtle and complicated relationships between the various parts of a living organism, and between the organism and its environment. For this argument, as we have already seen, the most significant of these scientific patterns is the evolutionary theory in its widest sense. All the sciences contribute to it from astronomy, mathematics and physics to chemistry, botany and biology, and what the astronomer finds at one point and the biologist at another is part of a total consistency. The web of evolution links together the most ancient star and yesterday's new-born infant. Step by step, in causal relationships, through millions of years, from stellar gas and dust, to the formation of galaxies and planets, including our earth, to the emergence of living creatures and to *Homo sapiens*, the pattern has slowly been moulded and continues to take shape. And the inner shape of the evolutionary process is, I have argued, mind and self-awareness.

With the emergence of man and the rich intellectual and cultural life which mind has enabled him to develop, evolution becomes the concern of the historian, whose field of study is the development of human life and human institutions. And the centre of the historical web, its inner shape as disclosed by the biblical revelation, is unity and reconciliation. For the inner shape of biblical history is a microcosm of the inner shape of universal history.

Mind and self-awareness; unity and reconciliation : these are the great structural lines of the universal pattern. This contention will seem the most unwarranted optimism if we merely look back upon the past, but in the vast time-scale of nature and of history man's evolution is in its infancy. The full possibilities of his mind and self-awareness lie in the future. He has only taken a few hesitant steps towards unity and reconciliation, but the future stages of his evolution may well bring about a startling transformation.

When man emerged and began to use his distinctively human powers another 'change of state' began to occur in the evolutionary process. Now the infinitely slow workings of natural selection, the biological changes, the adaptations to environment became slight. The development of man's mental powers, the building up of his social life, of his civilization and his culture became rapid and widespread. As Julian Huxley wrote :

> The main unit of evolution in the human phase is not the biological species, but the stream of culture, and genetic advance has taken a back seat as compared with changes in the transmissible techniques of cultural advance—arts and skills, moral codes and religious beliefs, and, above all, knowledge and ideas.[1]

This has been a major theme of Sir Julian's writings over many years. He has been severely criticized by those biolo-

[1] *Evolution in Action* (1953), p. 17.

gists who hold that it is unscientific to reflect upon a possible philosophical truth to be discerned in the workings of nature, and still more unscientific to make a value judgment about the status of man in the process of evolution. These are narrowly conceived criticisms of a teaching which can be a significant connecting rod between the central pattern in science and the fundamental theme of the biblical revelation.

Mind is the inner shape of the evolutionary process, and now it has risen to the surface in the fullness of its power. This is what we are witnessing in the second half of the twentieth century. We see it perhaps most clearly in the astonishing advance of science and technology, and in the mastery of large-scale planning and administration. We may hope to see it in a new renaissance of the arts, philosophy and religion. This dominance of mind and our mastery over nature means, of course, that the pattern of evolution is in our hands. In the words of Genesis, man has been given dominion. It is a proud status, but it means that many forces, striving within millions of individual men and women, will be at work to shape the future. Man is a strange creature to be given such opportunity and power. He is compounded of intellect, for ever asking questions and seeking answers, and of imagination capable of tremendous flights into the unknown. He has a personal memory, and the memory of his collective past, enshrined in history, to guide him. Yet he is capable today, as always, of suicidal folly and deliberate cruelty. He is not only a self-conscious being; he is also a self with an unconscious which is a kind of seed-bed composted of heredity and environment, training and experience. The desire to love and the desire to hate, the lust for power and the longing for reconciliation, the noble aspirations and the evil purposes all grow here. This is the creature to whom dominion has been given.

What kind of world will men create in the future? We can

be reasonably certain that for some communities at least, and perhaps for all, it will be technologically efficient; a world of affluence and leisure. But what kind of human relationships between individuals, between classes, between nations, will be fashioned? It is at this point that we may turn for guidance to the historians.

Those who study history will not be so rash as to predict the future course of events. What they can do is to call the past in evidence. There was a time in the nineteenth century when progress, even inevitable progress, was thought to be the great structural line of history. The catastrophes and the attendant barbarities of the past fifty years—one of the cruellest periods in history—have destroyed that optimistic forecast of events. Progress in the past there has been; progress in the future we may hope for, but it is never inevitable. It is not a law of history : it must be hardly won by the intelligent use of power. Thus historians are inclined to see politics as the organizing principle which gives coherence to history, and politics and power are inextricably mingled, the one with the other. The art of politics is to obtain power, to keep it, and to know how to use it.

At first sight it might seem that the outer shape of history, which is the pursuit of power in all its forms, and the inner shape, which is unity and reconciliation, are totally opposed to each other. This is not necessarily so. To be alive is to exercise power. The more a man's life is directed by deliberate purposes, the more he will be compelled to face conflict and to exercise power. The purposes of a complex society are elaborate and demand an elaborate and sophisticated use of power. It is significant that the men in the Bible who believed most passionately in unity and reconciliation were political realists who used their own forms of power. Isaiah put political pressure upon the kings of Judah, and proclaimed his faith in the saga of Abraham during the years of the Assyrian aggression. Jesus wielded spiritual power as he proclaimed the kingdom of God to a politically divided nation in which rival groups struggled for mastery. These men saw the inner shape of history in the context of power politics.

The outer and the inner shape of history begin to come closer together when we recognize the way in which societies handle the problem of power. It is easy to fall into the trap of thinking that 'power' and 'power politics' are dirty words. They call up a mental picture of the ruthless rulers; the tyrants who 'wade through slaughter to a throne, and shut the gates of mercy on mankind'. We think of the battlefields of history and in our imagination we hear the tramp of armies and see the smouldering villages, the ruined cities and the long lines of dispossessed refugees. All this destruction, horror and misery, we think, because one man, or a group of men, lusted after power. Such uses of power were commended by the second Chancellor of the Republic of Florence between the years 1498 and 1513, whose name has passed into our common speech. He was Niccolò Machiavelli. His advice to rulers, based upon his admiration for Cesare Borgia, is given in his best-known work, *The Prince*, published in 1518.

> You must realize that there are two ways to fight. In one kind the laws are used, in the other, force. The first is suitable to men, the second to animals. But because the first often falls short, one has to turn to the second. Hence a prince must know perfectly how to act like a beast and like a man.[1]

When Machiavelli looked round upon the contentious peninsula of Italy he complimented himself upon his realism. Politics, as he saw them, are beyond, or rather below, moral good and evil. They have their own laws against which it is useless to protest. Yet it was a sad and bitter realism. 'If all

[1] *The Prince*, ch. 18.

men were good,' he wrote, 'these precepts would not be good.' We, looking round upon the history of our world in the last half century—fifty years which have seen the slaughter of two world wars, the extermination of six million Jews in Nazi-occupied Europe, the releasing of the atomic bomb on Hiroshima, and the mass liquidation of peasants in Soviet Russia—we, contemplating such events, may conclude that men with power 'know perfectly how to act like a beast'.

Machiavelli said that he appreciated 'that flavour which history possesses'. Other historians have detected a different flavour.

> It is by the combined efforts of the weak, made under compulsion, to resist the reign of force and constant wrong, that, in the rapid change but slow progress of four hundred years, liberty has been preserved, and secured, and extended, and finally understood.[1]

When societies have suffered from the misdeeds of their rulers they have opposed tyranny by setting up checks and counter checks against the abuse of political power. They have appealed to ancient usage, to long-established customs, and on the basis of these they have framed, and struggled to enforce, laws which are binding upon the ruler no less than upon the subject. The beast must learn to act like a man. In the western tradition they have also reacted by dividing power into balancing fractions, so that the government is confronted by an opposition, Employers' Federations by Trade Unions. Again, in the western tradition, they have divided power by making the authority of the Courts of Justice independent of the centres of political and economic power.

These have been the practical reactions against the tyrant —the enforcement of the rule of law and the balancing of

[1] Lord Acton, *Lectures on Modern History* (1921 ed.), p. 51.

power by dividing it. Societies also build up a more abstract defence. Slowly they frame a conception of justice, which is a definition of the relationships which ought to exist between different individuals or different groups within a community. In theory, though not always in practice, a system of justice ensures equality for all men before the law, and certain inalienable rights for all men. These rights have been defined many times; by Tom Paine and by the makers of the French Revolution, in the American Declaration of Independence, and, in 1948, in the United Nations Declaration of Human Rights.

This is the general pattern of political development at least in western civilization. It is a slow, erratic and fitful process because it seeks to control self-centred, self-willed, energetic and masterful people. Plotted on a graph it would show violent downward swings and much more gradual ascents. At any particular time the development reaches different points in different communities: the leadership and the driving force passes from one group to another. Yet over the years men learn to check arbitrary power by appealing to custom and to law, and by developing and refining their concept of justice.

Justice, protecting and enlarging liberty, is the point at which the outer and the inner shape of history begin to fit together like the external and internal walls of a room. Justice is the soil in which unity and reconciliation grow, and without it these virtues soon wither and die. That is why the Hebrew prophets, who saw reconciliation as the inner shape of history, demanded social justice in the name of God. A nation split down the middle by extremes of wealth and poverty was unreconciled within itself, and unfit to be an instrument of reconciliation. Therefore, 'let justice roll down like waters, and righteousness as an ever-flowing stream' (*Amos* 5.24).

RECONCILIATION AS PARTNERSHIP

Reconciliation is a word of vital importance in the development of personal relationships, and a word of rich meaning in Christian theology. It describes that act of loving relationship which, turning its back upon an unhappy past, moves towards another in understanding, generosity and self-sacrifice. It involves the denial of our pride, and the affirmation of our common human frailty. For Christians this movement in love towards one who is estranged is born of faith in God's act of reconciliation.

> When anyone is united to Christ, there is a new world; the old order has gone, and a new order has already begun.
> From first to last this has been the work of God. He has reconciled us men to himself through Christ, and he has enlisted us in this service of reconciliation (*II Cor.* 5.17-18).

The practical out-working of reconciliation in political affairs is to be found in the concept of partnership, which is defined by M. A. C. Warren as 'sharing with another or with others in action'.[1] Partnership, Dr Warren argues, is constituted of three factors. The first is genuine involvement. For instance, an advanced technological nation does not enter into partnership with an emergent African nation merely by making monetary loans available on reasonable terms. There must be a committal of both partners, each to the other, in trust, and this committal must preserve the identity of both. All this presupposes the second factor which is the acceptance of long-term responsibility. A shared enterprise cannot be entered into for a limited time and with nicely calculated commitments. It depends upon a willing agreement to enter into partnership and a willing agreement, when the time comes, to end it. The third factor is the readiness to pay the price of partnership, to accept all the limitations and liabili-

[1] *Partnership: the Study of an Idea* (1956), p. 12f.

ties which arise. Involvement of this kind must preserve the freedom of both partners : there can be no question of an enforced take-over. None the less, reconciliation in the field of politics requires a moral restraint upon freedom of action. Adlai Stevenson once said :

> We shall have to listen as well as talk; learn as well as teach. And I sometimes think that what America needs more than anything else is a hearing aid. We can encourage the acceptance of our ideas only as we are willing to accept the ideas and suggestions of others. All this means a large relinquishment of our freedom of action.[1]

In commending reconciliation in political action, a world-wide partnership based upon involvement with each other, and a willing acceptance of burdens and restraints, we are a long way from the bitter pessimism of Machiavelli and the cynicism of some of our contemporaries. They prefer a philosophy of despair to a philosophy of hope. The completely objective thinker, they declare, will be a thorough-going agnostic on all questions, because without agnosticism, distortion and inaccuracies must occur. We must choose between this kind of cynicism which refuses commitment and the Christian virtues of faith, hope and love. It is probably the most important choice which we must make. Men, taken as a whole, are not cynics : rather they 'abound in hope'. The Italian historian Benedetto Croce began an essay entitled *International Justice* by recognizing that political decisions are not normally operated by moral considerations, but by the interests of the strongest states or the most powerful unions. He then continued :

> And yet mankind does not renounce its longing and its demand for a more just, more gentle and more civilized world, that is, for a more human world, in which all rights will be protected; in which every good deed will find help

[1] Quoted from Warren, *Partnership*, p. 33.

and encouragement; in which hardships and sorrows will gradually diminish or will be transferred to a higher plane than cutting each other's throat; in which war will be abolished, not the metaphysical war which is inherent in life itself, but the war which continues the barbaric custom of bloodshed, massacres, cruelties and torments. Nor does mankind renounce its insistence and its hopes that the states will become the intermediaries and the instruments of this better world and will accept among their tasks and place above other tasks that of civilization, elevating themselves to 'ethical states' or 'states of culture'. This civilization and culture is so closely bound up with the conditions prevailing throughout the entire world that it cannot be safeguarded or promoted except by an international policy, also based on civilization and culture.[1]

The building up of unity and reconciliation within each society, in international relationships, and within the Christian Church (to its shame as unreconciled as any institution), is man's supreme task in the years which lie ahead. Certainly the process will be as slow and as subject to frustration as has been the progress of that justice, as yet limited and incomplete, for which man has striven so long. A reconciled world is the very heart of the biblical revelation. It is God's promise, but the emergence of this inner pattern as the outer shape of future history is not automatic or inevitable, any more than the responsible use of our minds and our self-awareness is automatic. The shape of things to come will be determined less by technology and comprehensive planning than by the fundamental attitudes of men towards each other. There is an equal possibility of growing conflict or of growing unity. The future is open-ended. Man will choose his own path, but this does not mean that there is no pattern in history except the one we impose upon it, and that the concept of a divine purpose for the world can be dismissed as an irrelevance.

[1] *Politics and Morals* (1946), p. 132.

GOD'S ACTION IN HISTORY

When, on the death of Mary Tudor, her sister Elizabeth ascended the throne on November 17th, 1558, ardent Protestants saw in the miraculous preservation of their Queen during all the turmoil of Mary's reign 'the admirable work of God's own hand'. For example, in an oration written for Elizabeth's accession John Hales told the Queen that she was 'of God specially sent and ordained'. He then imagined the deity speaking to the English people.

> Ye see, my people, what I have done for you . . . I have not only discovered mine, yours, and my land of England's enemies . . . but I have also taken away their head and captain, and destroyed a great number of them, that ye should not be troubled with them; and some of them I have left, that ye may make them spectacles and examples, to the terror and fear of their posterity.[1]

This is an example of the popular market-place belief in divine intervention in human affairs. It is the 'angels at Mons' theory of history, widely held, still preached in sermons, made respectable by classical Greek drama, and embedded in the liturgy of the Church. In the moment of supreme crisis, when man's policies have created an impossible predicament, God intervenes miraculously to establish the right and to protect his own people.

This popular belief of Church and State and market-place that God *intervenes* in history must be discarded, as we must discard the equally popular view that he intervenes in the natural order of the universe. God does not make occasional forays into historical situations, any more than he makes occasional forays into the realms of physics or biology.

On the other side of the coin is a different view of divine intervention. In this theory God at times injects into an

[1] J. E. Neale, *The Age of Catherine de Medici* (1963), p. 203.

historical situation a powerful force to scourge unrighteous nations; even one's own nation when it has disobeyed the divine will. It was an explanation of events used by the prophet Isaiah when Assyria threatened Judah.

> Ah, Assyria, the rod of my anger,
> the staff of my fury!
> Against a godless nation I send him,
> and against the people of my wrath I command him,
> to take spoil and seize plunder,
> and to tread them down like the mire of the streets
>
> (*Isa.* 10.5-6).

In the same way Jeremiah, a hundred years later, explained the aggression of Babylon. But when the scourging is finished, God breaks the whip in pieces. Assyria and Babylon go the way of all proud empires.

In the 1920s and '30s this view of history was popular in certain circles as Communism grew in power. The Soviet Union was seen as God's instrument to punish the nations of the west for their political follies and social injustices. In this form the interpretation must be rejected. It was not God who gave overwhelming military and political strength to Assyria in the seventh century BC, or to Russia in the twentieth century AD. There is, however, as we shall see, a theological truth embedded in this popular notion, though it must be accurately expressed.

Pieter Geyl, the distinguished Dutch historian, in an essay on Ranke, the father of modern historiography, quotes from a letter written by Ranke to his brother in 1820.

> God lives and is observable in the whole of history. Every deed bears witness to him, every moment proclaims his name, but especially do we find it in the connecting line that runs through history.[1]

[1] P. Geyl, *Debates with Historians* (1962 ed.), p. 16.

According to Geyl, it was this conviction which lay behind Ranke's steadfast refusal to judge or to condemn historical characters, and formed his ideal to discover and to record 'what had really happened in the past'. The historian's task is to follow in God's tracks. There is, he said, 'the unutterable sweetness of sharing in the divine knowledge'.

Ranke, unlike John Hales, did not believe in divine intervention in history. For him, every event, every historical situation has its place in God's plan. This is the meaning of his famous remark that every epoch is 'immediate to God'. Pieter Geyl sums up his attitude in these words:

> Ranke's soul is flooded with reverence at the spectacle afforded by history, for it is all of God. Evil and destruction have their places in God's plan. Shall the human being who is permitted to cast a glance into the mystery presume to find fault? We are there beyond good and evil. God's triumph is assured, but it springs from the conflict of opposing principles.[1]

The weakness of Ranke's view of history is, of course, that it reduces, perhaps excludes altogether, the responsibility of individuals and communities in the historic drama. The great crimes of history, the colossal blunders, as well as the everyday injustices and follies, become morally neutral events; 'transactions and occurrences' as Ranke sometimes described them.

In the light of these conflicting theories what reflections can be made about God's action in history? In the first place I stress again the point that we meet the divine purpose whenever in our experience we come up against the elemental quality in human affairs. There is a rock of what history is, and the rock can neither be evaded nor overcome. There are sequences of cause and effect in history and, on a broad scale, they can be predicted. Aggression and injustice

[1] *Op. cit.*, p. 16.

breed aggression and injustice and, unless the sequence is broken in time by magnanimity, it ends in ruin. To go against the grain of history, to cut across God's tracks, is self-defeating. Human purposes which are opposed to God's purpose inevitably frustrate themselves. This is the truth behind the picturesque theory of God sending Assyrian troops to scourge Judah, or stirring up the Communist threat to punish western Europe and America. Injustice, violence and a failure in reconciliation are bound to be followed by disaster simply because historical realities are what they are. The social inequality of the kingdom of Israel which cut that nation into two unequal parts, one privileged and wealthy, the other oppressed and poor, was, according to the prophet Amos, inevitably followed by such national feebleness that total defeat by the Assyrians was bound to happen. 'They do not know how to do right . . . therefore an adversary shall surround the land' (*Amos* 4.10-11). And aggression and violence, no less than injustice, bring inevitable consequences. The words of Jesus, 'they that take the sword shall perish by the sword' are not a moral exhortation but a statement of historical fact.

There is a second reflection. God's action is not often to be seen on the surface of history. It works by hidden chain reactions deep below the surface. That is why Ranke spoke of finding God especially 'in the connecting line which runs through history'. But there are disclosure points where the hidden chain reactions break surface, and the purpose of unity and reconciliation is made plain. This, as I have suggested in chapter 6, is clearly to be seen in biblical history, but there is a particular reason for this. Biblical history is concerned with small nations which, though they pretended to themselves to be powerful, were in reality politically insignificant. It is history in miniature; often the history of individuals. Moreover the Israelites, unlike many peoples, had a peculiar faculty for reflecting upon their fate, of asking insistently why things happened to them. As a result the history they wrote is fully interpreted history in which is highlighted the disclosure points where the inner shape of events is revealed. It is more difficult to discern the pattern of unity and reconciliation in the history of Europe or in the global history of modern times. It may be, however, that future historians will point to the policy which gave independence to India, and to the process which transferred full political power and responsibility to the new states in Africa, as moments when the inner shape of history stands revealed, and reconciliation was at least within men's grasp.

History, as it is written by historians today, is not, for the most part, in miniature. It is about complicated sequences of events and men of leadership and vast power. It is, perhaps, inevitable because this is what the documents record, though recently an economic historian has complained that most English historians are snobs who write only about 'top people'.[1] History as it is written is about politics and about power, about worldwide trends and international crises; but history as it is lived is much more about personal relationships between individuals, about life lived in families, in villages, in one man businesses, in small cultural groups. It is about the struggle of individuals to live, and to live with their neighbours; about their quarrels and reconciliations, their hate, compassion and abiding sense of a bond uniting them. It is here in personal relationships, where history as it is lived really rests, that the disclosure points of God's action are most often to be discerned.

Man's real choice, to which all his other decisions contribute, is the choice between living within, or standing outside, the divine pattern of unity and reconciliation, and certain

[1] W. G. Hoskins, 'Harvest and hunger', *The Listener*, December 10th, 1964.

inevitable consequences flow from this moral decision. If we fail to refine and extend justice in our societies, if we choose rivalry instead of partnership, and continue to live disunited and unreconciled, then we shall run our heads against the rock of what history is. The rock of modern history is different from all other epochs because now we possess atomic weapons and vast technical resources, and our freedom will be shaped by the necessary answer of self-destruction. If, on the other hand, we accept the pattern of the universe and its great structural line, the mind of man will be directed by the divine spirit of reconciliation. Then there will be peace upon earth—

> peace . . . founded on truth, built according to justice, vivi-fied and integrated by charity, and put into practice in freedom.[1]

[1] *Pacem in Terris*, Encyclical Letter of Pope John XXIII (April 1963), Eng. ed., p. 61.

FOR FURTHER READING

1. SCIENCE

Arber, A., *The Mind and the Eye*, Cambridge 1954

Birch, L. C., *Nature and God*, SCM Press 1965

Hawkes, J., *A Land*, Cresset Press 1951

Huxley, J., *Evolution in Action*, Chatto and Windus 1953

Lyttleton, R. A., *The Modern Universe*, Hodder and Stoughton 1960

Raven, C., *Teilhard de Chardin*, Collins 1962

Sherrington, C., *Man on his Nature*, Cambridge (2nd ed.) 1951

Teilhard de Chardin, *The Phenomenon of Man*, Collins 1959

Weizsäcker, C. F. von, *The History of Nature*, Routledge 1951

2. HISTORY

Bloch, M., *The Historian's Craft*, University of Manchester Press 1959

Butterfield, H., *History and Human Relations*, Collins 1951

Carr, E. H., *What is History?*, Pelican 1964

Renier, G. J., *History: its Purpose and Method*, Allen and Unwin 1950

Geyl, Pieter, *Debates with Historians*, Fontana 1962

3. RELIGION

Mosley, N., *Experience and Religion*, Hodder and Stoughton 1965

Macmurray, J., *The Structure of Religious Experience*, Faber and Faber 1946

Richardson, A., *History, Sacred and Profane*, SCM Press 1964

Tillich, P., *The Courage to Be*, Fontana 1962

INDEX